FREEDOM IN THE PULPIT

A Vision for Growth in Preaching

Barbara Bate

DISCIPLESHIP RESOURCES

MATERIALS FOR GROWTH IN CHRISTIAN FAITH & LIFE

—— NASHVILLE, TENNESSEE ——

P.O. BOX 840 • NASHVILLE, TN 37202 • PHONE (615) 340-7068

A CONGREGATIONAL LEADERSHIP RESOURCE

Additional Titles:

Contemporary Worship for the 21st Century
Dan Benedict and Craig Miller
Don't Shoot the Horse (Till You Know How to Drive the Tractor)
Herb Mather
The Faith-Sharing Congregation
Shirley Clement and Roger Swanson

Available from Discipleship Resources.

Library of Congress Catalog Card No. 95-083447

ISBN 0-88177-152-X

Unless otherwise indicated, all scripture quotations are taken from the New Revised Standard Version of the Holy Bible.

DR152

Then Jesus said to the Jews who had believed in him,

"If you continue in my word, you are truly my

disciples; and you will know the truth,

and the truth will make you free."

John 8:31-32 (NRSV)

Acknowledgments

Among the many people who have brought me to this stage in my pilgrimage, I mention in particular these people:

- Fellow learners and teachers of preaching—at Drew University Theological School, Princeton Seminary, McCormick Seminary, the Chicago Doctor of Ministry Program in Preaching, Vanderbilt Divinity School, and the national Academy of Homiletics;

- Participants in seminars and workshops where these ideas have been developed—in Georgia, Illinois, Kansas, New York, Pennsylvania, Tennessee, Texas, and Washington;

- Colleagues and friends in the Congregational Leadership Team, the Worship Unit staff, and the Emmaus noon group in The General Board of Discipleship, whose prayers, laughter, encouragement, and insights have made this work more fun than I could have imagined;

- Pastors from the United Methodist Academy for Preaching, many of whom have shared their statements about "the freedom to preach" as contributions to the book;

- Partners in producing this book for Discipleship Resources—in particular, Debra Ball-Kilbourne, David Hazlewood, Sharon Anderson and Kathy Manor;

- Beloved friends in Edgehill United Methodist Church in Nashville, who continually show me that the local church is alive and thriving;

- My family, who walk the talk and make the trip worthwhile.

TABLE OF CONTENTS

INTRODUCTION

"Every one hundred and sixty eight hours." Those were the first words I heard from a friend who had agreed to talk with me about his experience of preaching in a local church. I had known him for several years as an intelligent person, a dedicated counselor, and a periodically interesting preacher. But until that moment I did not know that he saw preaching as a dead weight. It dragged down his spirit and it counteracted the other positive feelings he had about pastoral ministry.

After nearly a decade of teaching in seminaries and leading workshops and continuing education events for preachers, I know this man is not alone. His phrasing may not be typical of other preachers, but his experience of unending pressure to produce the next sermon has been a sad refrain from other pastors. I am haunted by my friend's words. They call out for a spiritual renewal that goes far beyond the traditional "how-to's" of sermon preparation. How can that renewal occur?

I am convinced that preaching can be a creative and enjoyable process rather than a boring routine or a procrastinator's nightmare. But for this to occur, a vision of preaching is needed that will strengthen new preachers and sustain those who are more experienced and at times more cynical about life in the local church. This writing is intended to develop just such a vision, for those who preach and for those who listen to, evaluate, and support the work of preachers.

Powerful and effective preaching comes into the worshiping community from a person who is a pilgrim, a theologian, and one of the *laos*—the whole Body of Christ. At its best, preaching not only describes but enacts the power of God to transform people. The gospel of Jesus Christ has the power to change lives. In the very hearing and absorbing of the good news of Jesus Christ, people create their own versions of this good news and carry it forward into the world. This experience suggests what I mean by the title of this book. *Freedom of the pulpit is an authentic and joyful connection of the human and the divine that is experienced in vital worship.* When freedom of the pulpit is offered and encouraged within a congregation, God's work is being done.

> **Freedom of the pulpit is an authentic and joyful connection of the human and the divine.**

To the Readers

This book is written with more than one audience in mind. It is intended to affirm those of you who preach full-time and those of you who have few opportunities in the pulpit; those new to preaching and those yearning for renewal. The book itself includes various contemporary voices in addition to this writer. Incorporated in script within the text are brief accounts by several dozen preachers, identified by their first names, who have experienced the freedom to preach. Other statements offer insights about preaching, leadership, and spirituality written by various contemporary writers. All these people form a cloud of witnesses, witnesses to the freedom of the gospel and the power of faithful preaching for changing lives.

> *Sometime ago I met a man who was a member of one of the first churches I served as a student pastor. We talked for a while and shared information about people in the church. Then he shocked me with a statement that I will never forget. "Do you know that you saved my life?" Of course, I had no idea what he meant. But he explained that at one point he was suffering from a very serious illness and depression, and that he had given up on life and had lost his will to live. He said that he came to church one Sunday and something that I said in the sermon had a very profound effect on him. It literally gave him the will and courage to keep going… After we departed I returned to my study and found a copy of the manuscript of that sermon in my files. On it I had written, "Bad sermon. No response or comment. Poor job." It was then that I realized that it wasn't me that saved his life, it was God working through something that I had said. I learned the valuable lesson that if we allow God to direct and guide us in our preaching, God can work miracles by taking even our weakest efforts and making them touch people's lives in ways we can never imagine.*
>
> *James*

If you are starting in your journey as a preacher, you will need more than a vision book. You will need to find people who challenge and care about you, people with whom to test your initial efforts and help discern your voice and your gifts as a communicator.

Whatever your particular location, you are affected by preaching and worship in relation to Christian community.

If you are a person who preaches regularly, insights from practicing pastors and spiritual leaders can help you discuss your hopes and struggles with other colleagues in ministry. You may find that you need to stretch the boundaries of your habits and routines, even the routines that have served you well in the past.

What cobwebs need to be swept aside to let in new light?

If you are an active worshiper in your local congregation, the book offers models for discussion and planning that will aid teamwork among lay and ordained persons in your own setting. The word *laos* refers to the whole people of God. Preaching in worship comes into and can build community through the energy and commitment of those who are "doers of the Word and not hearers only."

If you are a person who works with preachers locally or regionally, this book offers a framework for thinking about quality and continuing improvement among present and future congregational leaders.

Whatever your particular location, you are affected by preaching and worship in relation to Christian community. Your opinion matters in this process. I trust that you will offer it with care and confidence in the work of God for the people of God.

A Listener's Journey

The phrase "freedom in the pulpit" had been echoing in my mind for many years before I began the outline for this book. I felt intuitively that the issue of freedom was central in the most important preaching I had heard in my life. Throughout childhood and college years in Ohio, and in later moves to places such as Connecticut, Oregon, Illinois, and Scotland, I found myself gravitating toward congregations with strong preaching, music, and corporate worship. While a graduate student at Yale University I sang in the chapel choir, served as a student deacon, and became part of a group planning Thursday afternoon alternative worship services. As a student, then a teacher, then a student again, I was equally at home in church and in the classroom.

I loved good preaching, and I noticed that particular ideas, images, and stories would stay in my memory long after the original moment in worship. When I became a professor of communication and director of a program in women's studies, I tried to focus attention on equipping my students to speak carefully and honestly. I discovered that what I wanted was more than—and apparently different from—undergraduate teaching. I knew there had to be questions more important than "Is this on the exam?" and "Are you doing anything important in class today?"

I entered seminary as a part-time midcareer student, hoping to work with others who cared deeply about preaching in local churches. I found great delight in learning and celebrating with other people who were midcareer professionals on an unexpected pilgrimage. When I had the opportunity after several years to begin teaching in a seminary, I jumped at the chance. Teaching with preachers became my ministry. Over and over again I could see the spark of excitement when a preaching student came into the classroom on fire about what he or she was about to say. I *knew* that proclaiming the gospel of Jesus Christ was worth the effort.

In the midst of studying and teaching preaching, another image of freedom in the pulpit emerged from outside my own culture and tradition. Encountering and joining with several African American and multiracial churches, I have seen preaching, singing, dance, and prayer being celebrated as gifts and sources of powerful change among whole communities.

The past decade has brought forth in me a sense of urgency about the present and future of preaching and preachers. While delighting in the growth and enjoyment felt by many people who preach, I have heard an equal number of pastors report being blocked, burned out, or dried up in preaching ministry. There is ample evidence that the task of proclaiming "good news" can sometimes turn into a bad joke. I have heard regional church leaders recount their dismay at listening to the same supposedly "personal" sermon illustration from half a dozen different pastors. I have heard numerous conversations bemoaning the poor state of preaching in a given congregation or region or denomination. I have been accosted by people on planes, in offices, and in casual conversations who have volunteered their critiques of sermons that left them cold and disconnected from God.

Poor preaching is not intentional. No one *plans* to produce boredom or do damage while in the pulpit. Many people currently preaching in local churches are

> **No one *plans* to produce boredom or do damage while in the pulpit.**

not experiencing freedom inside or outside the pulpit themselves; so they cannot convey that freedom to anyone else. Some speakers entering the pulpit for the first time are frightened by the image of preaching because they connect it with scholarly lecturing rather than authentic conversation in a community. Some pastors feel stuck in preaching ruts, trying to remember why they wanted to work in a local church in the first place. The problem is real and is serious.

As a national agency staff member dealing with worship and preaching, I recognize that preaching is reported to be done ineffectively in many settings. I know, however, that bad news can swallow up the good. I have been blessed numerous times by sermons that caught fire and made a difference—sometimes in spite of imperfect language or faulty organization in the preacher's message. In light of this mixture of good and bad news, it seems appropriate to acknowledge both the risks and the joy of preaching ministry in the local church. Can we develop a sustaining vision for preaching and preachers? Can the task of preaching be more mutually satisfying and more faithful to the God we honor?

My unequivocal answer to both questions is *yes*. Faithful, honest preaching is capable of making a difference in the world, whether that world includes twenty

> **Faithful, honest preaching is capable of making a difference in the world.**

worshipers in a rural congregation or two thousand parishioners in a metropolitan church. Because the Christian gospel is the word made flesh, it is experienced in the meeting of actual persons in real time and space, hearing and telling stories that matter, stories they believe because they believe each other.

Whether or not a preacher has been trained for the task, he or she has the task of *stating a vision* for the congregation. The spiritual leadership of a community cannot simply emerge from prayer or committee work, or even from dedicated service in the local community. The vision needs to be articulated through personal and authentic communication, heard, seen, and felt in the gathered community. Parishioners hope for an engaging, irresistible vision that will send them forward into the world. If they do not hear the vision from a spiritual leader, they may continue to hope it will emerge somehow, but they are not as likely to be empowered to share that vision with other people and sustain it for themselves.

For preaching to become a joyful endeavor, those of you who p
part of a community, just as any Christian needs to be part of a fai
Opportunities to learn and grow are central to preaching effective
are beginning or continuing your journey into the pulpit. In order to gain or reg
the energy to speak an empowering word to others, you need to experience the
presence of others with whom you can speak of both your hopes and your struggles.
Only as you celebrate the grace of God in your own midst can you become a company of disciples working to equip other disciples. Norman Shawchuck and Roger
Heuser state the issue from a biblical perspective, noting that today's spiritual leaders need covenant communities just as the first century disciples did.

> One of the main reasons for living in covenant with a small
> group of other pastors or religious leaders is that *the community does
> your faith when you cannot do for it for yourself.* We should not take
> lightly the poignant words of Jesus to his community on the night
> of his deepest agony, "Pray for me." To whom can you confess your
> sins and lament your failures? With whom can you be in covenant
> around the temptations that beset you in ministry and the disci-
> plines you so sorely need—but cannot seem to master? With
> whom can you 'let your hair down' without fear of criticism?
>
> Norman Shawchuck and Roger Heuser, *Leading the Congrega-
> tion: Caring for Yourself While Serving Others*, Abingdon, 1993, p. 49.

Technique and Process

Many books on preaching offer techniques and tools for producing sermons on
the model of great "pulpiteers" of the past. But at the end of this century and the
dawning of another, great sermons of the past are not suitable examples for most
preachers to follow. Listeners often have expectations for preaching based more on
television comedies and talk shows than on written essays and public lectures. At
times people trying to improve their preaching conclude that jokes and proverbs
are the only way to keep people's attention during worship. Books of sermon illustrations and preprinted generic sermons imply
that the keys to preaching are cleverness and
general truths. But the truths that open the
gospel to its hearers come from voices that are
individual, current, and honest. Wherever you
are in your life and your vocational path, your
growth as a preacher is likely to emerge from
honoring—not denying—your own history,
tradition, and gifts. If you experience preaching
as a celebration of freedom in the gospel, your
own and others' worship experience will be more appealing, creative, and faithful
to the Jesus story.

Wherever you are in your life and vocational path, your growth as a preacher is likely to emerge from honoring—not denying—your history, tradition, and gifts.

Skill development in preaching, as in many other fields, is appropriate. It is no substitute, however, for grounding in the One who makes the effort worthwhile. Books, videos, periodicals, and workshops can mislead the new or the long-term preacher if they teach particular skills *apart* from the creative Spirit that comes uniquely into each person. In light of that conviction, this writing is not a product to be marketed as "great preaching for the next century." Instead I encourage you to *listen to the great preaching that you yourself can hear and do,* wherever you are located within the Body of Christ.

> **Listen to the great preaching that you yourself can hear and do.**

Commitments to Growth

Effective preaching in Christian worship is a primary way for a congregation to empower and equip disciples. Jesus used a variety of preaching styles and situations to affirm, educate, and challenge his followers. Contemporary preachers use whatever tools they can find to do the same. As you gather ideas and techniques for building skill and confidence for preaching ministry, you can remind yourself that the freedom to preach moves you into the realm of transformation—changing lives in light of the gospel, including your own life. Your responsibility, if you choose to accept it, involves four kinds of commitments. The four are summarized here and described more extensively later in relation to the four compass directions in the book.

First, if you are to preach, you need to **make a covenant to continue your own spiritual development** as a participant in an ongoing journey of faith. You cannot assume that seminary degrees, years of Bible study, or even daily devotional disciplines will automatically make your faith solid and unwavering. You will need to open yourself to change, questioning assumptions about what God is saying to you on a given Sunday morning (or Wednesday or Saturday evening). The journey is both intimate and public, lonely yet profoundly communal. It will take whatever shape your particular journey, talents, and struggles make available. You are likely to be surprised at times, and often placed beyond your zone of comfort.

Spirituality in preaching can be taken for granted. Pastors with many years experience report that their own spirituality can be lost in the pressure to get a sermon finished. The goal in this writing is to move away from the implied expectation that a given preaching event will be finite or complete. Life will go on beyond the words you speak.

The second commitment for effective preaching is **thoughtful preparation of yourself and the Word you are to share**. Listening is the prerequisite for keeping that commitment. You will need to listen to the world of *Scripture,* with its history and witness. You will need to listen to the *community* that surrounds your preaching, as it includes and goes beyond your immediate congregation. You will need to listen to the world of your own experience as *the preacher,* including the training, theological perspectives, and human relationships that filter through you as you prepare.

)n to preach entails purpose, form, and language. You will be process of discerning:

- what is worth saying,
- why you believe it,
- how to place ideas and experiences in memorable form, and
- what words come to life for you and others who encounter your preaching.

Tools for carrying out this discerning process are widely available. How you prepare will be guided by tradition, training, preference, and most of all by the Holy Spirit. With a perspective on preaching as a giving and receiving of a sacred gift, you may be released from the pressures brought on by perfectionism or desperation and allowed to experience your own God-given creativity.

The third commitment to freedom in the pulpit is to **be ready to encounter the Body of Christ within worship**. In order to encounter Christ's Body in worship you will need to recognize yourself as one who longs for the living Word of God. You are symbolically, if not actually, one of the people sitting expectantly in a front pew or lurking quietly in a corner at the rear. In order to be part of this encounter, a number of nonverbal behaviors can keep you attentive to the connection between your own experience and that of others. Careful eye contact, effective use of written materials when you need them, and the use of your own voice, movements, and gestures—all of these signal that you (the person in the pulpit) are a member of the family of God along with those in front of you.

> *In order to encounter Christ's Body in worship you will need to recognize yourself as one who longs for the living Word of God.*

The fourth commitment to freedom in the pulpit is a **covenant to treat yourself and other preachers as an ongoing community**. A single course or workshop will not make you a congregation of preachers, but you can find settings in which you are accountable to engage in an honest spiritual search. Some preachers have more resources for undertaking their spiritual and professional growth than others. You may already have a substantial library of materials on preaching and worship, or you may be isolated from continuing education programs, from seminaries, and even from others growing in their own preaching ministry. I have met lay and ordained preachers who are a hundred miles from their nearest colleagues. Both geography and schedules can make it almost impossible to get together for anything other than yearly meetings.

> *Growth is not an option; it is a necessity.*

Intentional, collegial learning is not easy. You will have particular challenges if you are in churches with smaller memberships, if you serve part-time, or if you work in multiple job settings. But growth is not an option; it is a necessity. You need and deserve regular opportunities to develop your spirituality, your skills, and your sense of the wider system of ministry of which you are a part. Your experience as a preacher is essential not only to you, but to the present and future leadership of Christian communities.

Tools for Learning

This book is intended to serve as a tool for continuing learning of individuals and groups in a variety of settings. The *desired results* for the book are ambitious.

First, I trust in your increasing *confidence and willingness to experiment and grow,* whether as a new or experienced preacher. The gift of creativity comes ultimately from God; but it can be nourished or squashed by the actions of human beings. Even dedicated professors of preaching can fail to recognize or affirm an approach that does not fit their own tradition or practice. If you are open to new ideas and perspectives you may discover a new energy for your own preaching.

Second, I count on the power of nourishment for the Body of Christ through *covenantal dialogue* among those who preach, a process often called Christian conferencing. Any spiritual leader risks isolation, discouragement, or cynicism when away from others who understand their experiences and challenge them to integrity and hope. Numerous pastors in mid-life have reported changing their minds about staying in ordained ministry because of honest, continuing encounters with their peers.

Third, I expect that spiritual and interpersonal growth among the company of preachers will result in *more challenging, visionary, and empowering preaching* in local congregations. No book or teacher alone can do this. But I believe in the biblical affirmation that God's word is intended to go forth and be fruitful in the world. The movement from Spirit to speaker to responding community does not have to be forced. It is natural and intentional as a part of God's work in the world. You can celebrate your part in that work.

> **Spiritual and interpersonal growth among the company of preachers will result in more challenging, visionary, and empowering preaching in local congregations.**

Continuing professional learning is typically done in three ways: individual study, plenary events, and small group process. The first two methods are currently the primary vehicles for continuing education for pastors and other spiritual leaders. The present book, along with other resources, is focused on the third option—small group learning—as an alternative that fosters both spiritual development and professional skill improvement.

Individual study is a long-honored means of learning. Hundreds of useful books, articles, periodicals, and audio or video resources are available to encourage your thinking about the topic of preaching. The value of this approach is in being able to focus on particular needs as you see them, while controlling your time as you pursue your own learning. The limitation lies in the nature of preaching as an interpersonal, intentional event of oral communication. It is impossible to hear and recognize your own voice or presence as a preacher without filtering through them your own biases or anxieties.

Plenary events, the second current option, bring together experts and adult learners with particular insights and energy for encouraging growth in preaching. The importance of the topic to many people and the stature of a national expert can contribute to the experience. The long-term results of such events are limited, however, because of a lack of carryover between the event and the ongoing needs of local congregations and their leaders. It is hard to remember what you thought was a wonderful idea more than a year ago.

Small group learning is the third alternative lifted up in this book. It is an idea related to the Wesleyan class meeting and the covenant discipleship group, since these small groups are intended to build support and accountability over time. Small groups are in evidence in various parts of the church, but until recently they have not been cited as a major factor in the literature on preaching and congregational leadership. The reasons are several. Until recently, most traditional courses in homiletics focused on the individual's skilled performance of single sermons rather than the long-term development of congregational leaders. Furthermore, the dominant culture in the United States prides itself on individual success and fosters avoidance of group situations that could reveal participants' inadequacies in a task as essential as preaching the gospel. Perhaps the most telling reason for the absence of small group opportunities for many preachers is that many of the people involved have seen themselves as *enabling the growth of others rather than being called by God into their own growth and transformation.* It is hard for a helper to ask for help without seeming lazy or selfish.

> *Perhaps the most telling reason for the absence of small group opportunities for many preachers is that many of the people involved have seen themselves as enabling the growth of others rather than being called by God into their own growth and transformation.*

Happily, a shift is taking place among many laypersons and clergy, leading to a more mutual commitment to growth in preaching and worship. Hundreds of people who have engaged in lectionary study groups, clergy-lay worship planning groups, and ministerial support groups recount positive experiences and an increasing sense of partnership. Within the church as a national and international organization, this book is one of a number of continuing efforts to focus attention on quality in congregational leadership. We have been looking for ways to support spiritual leaders for congregations and regional church bodies, recognizing that the issues in one denomination are likely to parallel those in others as well. Our goal is to help develop and sustain future leadership in Christian communities. The effort involves a variety of learning methods and media. In addition to this book two series of teaching videos by preaching experts have been produced recently (*Staying ALIVE in the Pulpit*, Series One and Two)[1]. Behind all of this work is the belief that people who lead congregations are first of all *persons*, children of God who need attention and care as they grow and change.

> *People who lead congregations are first of all persons, children of God who deserve attention and care as they grow and change.*

The framework for FREEDOM IN THE PULPIT as a whole and the segment "Breathing the Spirit" deal especially with spiritual growth. The segments "Preparing the Word" and "Encountering the Body of Christ" offer insights for increasing your professional skills as effective communicators in worship. The remaining segments, "Sustaining the Community" and "Navigating the Future," give particular

---

[1] Presenters in Video Series One are Zan W. Holmes, Jr., David Buttrick, Virginia Pharr, and Thomas Troeger. Presenters in Series Two are Heather Murray Elkins, Paul Scott Wilson, Eugene Lowry, and David Schlafer. Both series are available through Discipleship Resources and EcuFilm.

attention to ways that preachers can grow as a community of learning leaders and increase the quality of spiritual leadership throughout the church and the world.

This book is a finite object, but its goal is not the production of a completed statement. Like the preaching issues and processes to be considered here, FREEDOM IN THE PULPIT is intended to have results beyond itself. It is my hope that the stories, images, and insights included here will extend beyond any sentence, paragraph, or quotation included in these pages. It is hard to talk about a changing process in traditional terms—words, sentences, and paragraphs. This is one reason that the book includes a variety of voices within its pages. For example, organizational consultant and writer Margaret Wheatley suggests something of the quality of living in a world of radical shifts in our thinking, based on the radical shift from particles to waves in quantum physics. In keeping with her words, you are invited to be open and inventive as you respond to the rest of these pages.

> To be responsible inventors and discoverers . . . we need the courage to let go of the old world, to relinquish most of what we have cherished, to abandon our interpretations about what does and doesn't work. . . . We must learn to see the world anew. . . . To live in a quantum world, to weave here and there with ease and grace, we will need to change what we do. We will need to stop describing tasks and instead facilitate process. We will need to become savvy about how to build relationships, how to nurture growing, evolving things.
>
> Margaret Wheatley, *Leadership and the New Science,*
> Berrett Koehler, 1992, pp. 5, 38.

A Reflection Exercise

This exercise is an opportunity to examine your assumptions about typical, ideal, or problematic preaching. The words and phrases listed on page 11 were generated from a word association exercise during a national meeting of regional directors of lay speaking. Seventy people involved in congregational and Annual Conference leadership were invited to share their word associations for the word "preaching." As you can see from the lists, some of the same items were seen as positive by some and negative or neutral by others.

Examine these lists.

1. Which features or qualities do you identify as positive for preaching in general?
2. Which are typical of your own preaching?
3. Are there words or phrases that represent controversial areas, or items about which you or others are uncertain?

Positive Associations	Negative Associations	Either + or -
Inspiring	Boring	Challenging
Teaching	Wordy	Three Points
Sharing	Not Relevant	Manuscript
Expectant	Rambling	Performing
Caring	Pointless	Delivery focus
Responsibility	Lecture	Technique focus
Storytelling	Poorly prepared	Twenty minutes
Creativity	Judgmental	Theatrical
Message	Current events	
Biblically based	One man show	
Prophetic	Gutless	
Entertaining	Insensitive	
Twenty minutes		
Worldwide		
Urging commitment		
Purpose		
Altar call		
Loving		
Individualized		
Inviting		
Emotional		

What words or phrases would you add for your own list of preaching associations?

CHAPTER 1:
A VISION OF FREEDOM

As a seminary student in my first preaching course, I worked hard on my first sermon. I walked anxiously toward the pulpit—not a traditional pulpit at all, but a lectern in a crowded studio used for videotaping. I was anxious about my ability to do this important task well. I had experienced a call to work with preachers in the future; I knew I needed to be a credible performer in the pulpit in order to realize that future goal. I had done my exegesis, organized the message, practiced several times, and truly liked the passage assigned to the class, the account of the Transfiguration in Matthew 17:1-9. Despite all this effort, and despite my many years of speaking in front of other people, I was extremely nervous, much more than I had expected. *This moment counted*, and I might do a bad job!

Suddenly, as I finished reading the Scripture and moved into the first words of the sermon, I felt changed. I was no longer a public speaker doing a performance in front of judges; I was an honored guest at a celebration, with Jesus as the host. The physical sensations of shaking fingers, flushed cheeks, and wobbly legs were replaced with what I can only call an awe-filled exhilaration. I had a chance to tell the best story of all! The gift of this opportunity has remained with me as one of the central images in my life. I am reminded of it nearly every time I preach. I continue to experience the joyfulness that can come into and through worship. *Freedom in the pulpit is a gift from God.*

I have shared this story with people who have been preaching for many years. Many of them have responded with their own stories of intense anxiety and equally strong memories of the power of that first preaching moment. Here is one account:

> *The first time I was asked to preach, I was a freshman in college… I was one nervous wreck. I entitled my sermon, "Jesus, The Way, The Truth, and The Life." When I finished, I not only felt relief, but I realized that I had attempted to preach the whole gospel in one sermon—and that in twelve minutes time.*
>
> *Charlotte*

However it is phrased, the freedom given by God can open up the one who proclaims the good news while it liberates the ones who receive the Word. Preaching matters, and it works on the preacher as much as on anyone.

Scriptural Examples of Freedom

Though the word *freedom* is not the most frequent term used in the Bible, the *experience of freedom* is woven through Scripture and the history of Christian communities. Beginning with his first recorded preaching in Nazareth, Jesus stated a vision of freedom—from blindness, from captivity, from oppression.

"The Spirit of the Lord is upon me,
because he has anointed me to bring good news to the poor.
He has sent me to proclaim release to the captives
and recovery of sight to the blind, to let the oppressed go free,
to proclaim the year of the Lord's favor."
And he rolled up the scroll, gave it back to the attendant, and sat down.
The eyes of all in the synagogue were fixed on him.
Then he began to say to them,
"Today this scripture has been fulfilled in your hearing." (Luke 4:18-21, NRSV)

Freedom is offered to those who have ears to hear and are willing to respond. In the Lucan story, of course, the listeners heard more than they expected. They did not like the kind of freedom that challenged their view of themselves. Freedom in the Scriptures includes risk. The same is true of freedom in the contemporary church and the world at large. Yet even with the risk, there is a great deal of evidence that the gospel's good news for humanity invites disciples into a freedom that can be irresistible. Three dimensions of this freedom are especially important in thinking about preaching:

- *freedom as vision,*
- *freedom as worship,* and
- *freedom as community.*

Freedom as Vision

In Joel 2:28-29, God offers a spiritual vision for all of God's children:

> Then afterward I will pour out my spirit on all flesh;
> your sons and your daughters shall prophesy,
> your old men shall dream dreams,
> and your young men shall see visions. (NRSV)

In Revelation 21:10, the holy city of God becomes a vision for the eternal future:

> And in the spirit [the angel] carried me away to a great, high mountain
> and showed me the holy city Jerusalem coming down out of heaven from
> God. (NRSV)

Freedom as Worship

In Isaiah 55:12, the whole creation turns into a worship event:

> For you shall go out in joy, and be led back in peace;
> the mountains and the hills before you shall burst into song,
> and all the trees of the field shall clap their hands. (NRSV)

In John 4:23-24, Jesus offers the Samaritan woman true worship, going beyond past rules and constraints:

> But the hour is coming, and is now here, when the true wor-
> shipers will worship the Father in spirit and truth, for the Father
> seeks such as these to worship him. God is spirit, and those who
> worship God must worship in spirit and truth. (NRSV)

Freedom as Community

The Exodus story shows the literal movement from bondage to freedom through continuing spiritual leadership, as evidenced in Exodus 12:50-51:

> All the Israelites did just as the Lord had commanded Moses and
> Aaron. That very day the Lord brought the Israelites out of the
> land of Egypt, company by company. (NRSV)

John 8:31-32 shows Jesus reminding the disciples that they will be a sacred community even though Jesus himself will not be with them:

> If you continue in my word, you are truly my disciples; and you will
> know the truth, and the truth will make you free. (31b, NRSV)

The Bible shows God empowering people and transforming their lives at the core. The word of God is active, in and through the people of God. The gospel is a story capable of moving both worshipers and preachers from captivity of any sort toward liberation into new and more abundant life.

Liberation, Not License

Biblical freedom is liberation—from prejudice, from fear, and from impairments both literal and figurative. This freedom ranges from an individual's release from psychological trauma (the Gerasene demoniac in Luke 8:26-39) to a community's realization of joyful interdependence (The Acts of the Apostles, chapters 2 and 4). But freedom in the Christian gospel is quite different from the libertarian view that depicts freedom as the absence of accountability. Freedom has sometimes been portrayed to people outside the United States as the honoring of each individual. What is called freedom in much of secular North American culture, however, is the expression of any personal preference, and thus a license by some individuals or groups to ignore the rights and experiences of others. This may be why the title of this book sometimes brings a chuckle or an exclamation of surprise. In a predominantly secular context the phrase "freedom in the pulpit" connotes the opportunity to say anything the preacher pleases.

A biblical understanding of freedom is that God brings people into a more liberated and liberating vision of themselves, their communities, and the world as they become disciples of Jesus Christ. One modern statement about Christianity and creation places human beings in the active center of the family of God, accountable for their lives and able to act together in behalf of freedom.

> The human being is called to be creator and participator in the work of God's creation. It is God's call addressed to human beings toward which they must respond freely. God does not need submissive and obedient slaves, always trembling and egotistically preoccupied with themselves. God needs sons and daughters, free and creative, loving and daring.
>
> Nicholas Berdyaev, "Salvation and Creativity: Two Understandings of Christianity," quoted in John Culley and Kristi Culley, *Be Not Conformed: Changing the Way We See the World*, Meyer Stone, 1989, p. 60.

Two other statements about freedom have come from pastors living in different parts of the United States. As they indicate, freedom in the pulpit can be both an *internal response* by the preacher and a *corporate decision* by a congregation.

> *I do not know when it happened. Try as I might, I cannot verify the exact date. I just know that I awoke one morning and realized that, while Bishops, District Superintendents and local church leaders were still important and to be respected, no one other than myself could take the honor or the blame for my preaching. That's freedom!*
>
> *Danny*

*The 'free pulpit resolution' of the First Methodist Episcop
Church, Evanston, Illinois, was written in 1933 in respon
conflict over the pastor's expressed views about war and
It includes these words: "We stand for a free pulpit and d
church. We do not expect or desire a minister simply to ec..
the opinions of the congregation, and we do not assert our
individual agreement with all our minister's utterances. But we
vigorously resent the effort of outside organizations to dictate
to the church or to prescribe its message."[2]*

Dwight

The statements describe two different but compatible perspectives. The second statement is important as an example of a church's history. The predominant concern of this book, however, is suggested in the first statement, focusing on the freedom of the pulpit as the preacher's experience of becoming a disciple and spiritual leader.

Preaching and the Congregation's Task

Christian ministry occurs in and through local congregations. People experience freedom to live abundantly and to participate in efforts of love and justice. The flow of ministry into, through, and beyond the local church has four elements:

1. Reaching out and receiving people, wherever they are and whatever their circumstances.
2. Helping people to grow in relating to God.
3. Nurturing people in community and equipping them for discipleship.
4. Sending people into the world as active and loving disciples of Jesus Christ.

These four elements are in a continuous flow of ministry. The ministry of the church exists beyond itself, giving itself away for a world that is loved by God and meant to be served through the people of God.

> **Preaching and worship are central to the flow of ministry in the local church.**

Preaching and worship are central to the flow of ministry in the local church. Effective and faithful preaching in worship can increase that flow. For purposes of this discussion you can look at them one at a time while realizing that they are interrelated.

1. **Reaching out and receiving people** can occur in the welcome given to visitors and regular worshipers by both laypersons and worship leaders, including the preacher. As a preacher, you can use language that *approaches* hearers rather than putting them off or putting them down. "I-you" pronouns, for example, can convey a climate of conversation or dialogue rather than a formal announcement or lecture. Preaching and other features of worship can open the door of welcome, offering immediate and profound symbols of God's hospitality toward humanity. How you preach can also stretch the imaginations of the receivers of the Word as

---

[2] Dwight R. Bastian, "A Homiletical Analysis of Ernest Fremont Tittle's Sermons on War and Peace from 1918 to 1949," STD dissertation, Garrett-Evangelical Theological Seminary, 1975, p. 9.

> **Preaching and other features of worship can open the door of welcome, offering immediate and profound symbols of God's hospitality toward humanity.**

well, encouraging those gathered to think about other individuals and communities as children of God—AIDS patients, homeless people, children who are afraid, elderly people without support.

2. <u>Helping people in relating to God.</u> Relating people to God is not the same thing as talking about God. People can hear lectures about the power of God without feeling connected to the divine and loving presence in their own lives. The difference lies in the distinction between *spiritual formation* and *theological information*. Even when the worship service at a particular church lacks perfection in its details, the work of the Holy Spirit can come forth in the voice and face and caring of the one who brings the Word. Information about God becomes worthwhile for people when it is used in formation and celebration of life in the Spirit. Preachers and worship leaders do not control the Spirit, but they can honor and delight in its presence in worship. Unfortunately, some listeners to sermons come away from worship with a kind of guilty disappointment: "It was an interesting talk, but I wasn't sure what was supposed to happen to me." People are willing to be impressed by pulpit speaking. When they are intimidated rather than fed they may believe it is their fault. It is not! Preachers have the gift and the responsibility of being *matchmakers*: helping to wed the crucial encounter of humans' yearnings with God's outrageous love.

3. <u>Nurturing in community and equipping for discipleship.</u> Preaching may not appear to be a communal act, yet it is. Preaching is sacred conversation among the people, the proclaimer, and God. How you affirm or ignore the people present as a potentially growing community of disciples will affect whether or not the worshipers believe they are part of the Body of Christ.

In the church of my childhood, there was much more talk from the pulpit about personal piety than about possibilities for community and support for each other. This fed my belief that the Christian faith was essentially a matter of living up to a high standard of private morality. When I went to worship or Sunday school, I participated in a school as competitive as my weekday school. Individual and private morality were the only keys to that realm; not until later did I discover communities of people who would support, challenge, and stick by each other. Being a Caucasian, Northern European American may have been another constraint, for I have since come to know African Americans, Hispanics, Native Americans, and Asian Americans who have a vital sense of mutuality and discipleship in their congregations.

4. <u>Sending people forth into the world as disciples.</u> The self-contained congregation cannot be the church of Jesus Christ for the world. Disciples need to be people who know who they are, what they believe, and how their actions interrelate with forces of good or evil around them. The image of the church as a fortress is changing to the image of a community in mission to its surroundings. Daily ministry comes through each person who has been encountered by the living God.

An invitation to discipleship within a sermon is one obvious way to extend a local congregation's movement into mission. Many preachers, however, have found another way to embody the process of sending forth. They have done so simply by sharing authentic stories of grace and redemption that involve everyday people rather than distant or unreal heroes and heroines.

> **The image of the church as a fortress is changing to the image of a community in mission to its surroundings. Daily ministry comes through each person who has been encountered by the living God.**

THE FLOW OF MINISTRY

Through a spiritual leader's freedom to preach a faithful, creative, and joyous word, the Christian gospel becomes a conduit. The waters of baptism flow outward from the congregation into its surroundings, leading to an ever-increasing freedom of the people to celebrate God's love and justice throughout the world.

Nurturing in Discipleship

Relating to God

Sending Out Disciples

Reaching Out and Receiving

A vivid memory of a seminary preaching class involved Steve, a bright but quiet student who covered his fear of preaching with the statement, "I don't plan to preach; I'm going to be a church administrator." In his last preaching event for the year, he finally looked out from his manuscript for the first time. He told of his boyhood hometown and its importance to him as a parallel to the Old Testament community of his chosen Scripture. When he sat down, he immediately apologized for the "hokey" hometown reference. But others in the room exclaimed, *"But that was when I heard God!"* Steve thought he had failed, but the Word came to life when he allowed it to speak to his own life.

> **The preacher's job is not to beat others into submission, but to lift up the possibility of personal and corporate discipleship.**

To move from sermon to response—or more accurately from worship into the world—is to move toward empowerment and change. The preacher's job is not to beat other people into submission, but to lift up the possibility of personal and corporate discipleship. Discipleship can take as many forms as the numbers of persons who hear it. The core process is the movement from being a receiver to being a sharer and sender—from being a customer for a message from God to being a supplier of that continuing message to other people.

My hope in mentioning the congregation's task in the book is to remind all of us that *worship is corporate*, not individual. Even when one individual preaches, there is an interchange that can change those present—intentionally or unintentionally.

I borrowed a phrase from Max Lucado and built a sermon around it—"Anchor deep, say a prayer, and hold on." I attributed the phrase to him and then spent most of the sermon around how we do this. I was totally surprised when, over a year later, a father of a sick child from our congregation said, "The thing that got me through was when we decided to 'anchor deep, say a prayer, and hold on.'" I asked if he was quoting me or Max through me and he said—"Oh, yes, that was a from a sermon of yours last October!" I will never again believe that preaching doesn't matter or that people don't really listen. Words matter—and preaching can change lives.

Derf

Preaching in worship is an essential way, but by no means the only way, to receive people, or to show them community. It is a way of demonstrating in microcosm the ongoing flow of welcoming, forming, and sending forth disciples. Worship as a whole is *liturgy*. It is the work of the people offered by the *laos*—laypersons, pastors, and church professionals. Within that community the preacher is both a bridge to outsiders and a spokesperson for the gathered church. Worship and evangelism, in other words, are mutually supportive processes rather than competitors for the congregation's or community's attention. The preacher is part of the community, one who challenges and builds up the people rather than being a star performer on Sunday morning. Because people have many options for the use of their time, they are not likely to tolerate boredom, abuse, or irrelevance. They

> *Viewing preaching as a pilgrimage signals a paradigm shift for the preacher, listeners, and those who train and evaluate pastors.*

are very likely, however, to have a yearning for an empowering truth. Preaching can illuminate that truth and bring it into action.

The Preaching Pilgrimage: Journeying in Sacred Space

Viewing preaching as a pilgrimage can stretch some assumptions about time and space in the church. *The American Heritage Dictionary*, third edition, defines a pilgrimage as "a journey to a sacred place." The distinction between the terms *sermon* and *preaching* may not seem particularly important at this point, but I believe that viewing preaching as a pilgrimage signals a paradigm shift for the preacher, listeners, and those who train and evaluate pastors.

Preaching, in this perspective:
- is part of a worship experience that occurs in space and time;
- can include multiple persons in leadership and in the pews; and
- can have an impact extending far beyond the particular event through the memories, imaginations, and actions of others.

I once began a preaching workshop with the statement, "A sermon is not a thing." My intent was to jostle people away from the idea that a sermon is a perfectly written product which is composed and delivered, written to be copied onto pieces of paper and into the heads of an audience. That definition of *sermon* is based on a traditional linear model of communication, one assumed to be appropriate in many settings. A memo, a short story, a recipe, and this book can be taken as individual items in time and space which have finite starting and ending points. Without boundaries we would have trouble completing the tasks we undertake. Yet worship in the Christian community is intended to make a difference beyond itself, to bring together the finite and the infinite, and to open up the reign of God in our presence. How can we convey and experience the reality that lies behind our words?

Architecture professor Robert Harris of the University of Oregon once said in a lecture, "Design is a spin-off in the process of understanding." This unusual statement is a reminder that even in the world of concrete, steel, and bricks the architect is asked to be a continuing learner, to test (we would hope effectively!) concepts, materials, and images to fit a particular moment under particular constraints of time and space.

Preaching is not sheets of papers in a file cabinet, but a continuing series of processes —experiences that emerge first in the preacher and then become available for those in worship, and beyond. This idea is quite different from the textbooks on preaching that give rules such as the often-cited three points and a poem!

> *Preaching is not sheets of paper in a file cabinet, but a continuing series of processes—experiences that emerge first in the preacher and then become available for those in worship, and beyond.*

A rule can be a helpful discipline if it aids your thinking and allows for creativity. But many "rules" in preaching are no longer valid because worshipers are surrounded each day with quick bursts of sound and sight rather than extended patterns of reasoning. You do not have to be a peddler of the gospel to recognize that people's habits are affected by the ways they spend their time outside the local church.

Clock and Calendar, Kairos and Chronos

The clock and the calendar are natural parts of the pastor's or worship leader's equipment. Like many other people in organizations you are asked to pay attention to the immediate and larger time frames in which you are accountable. Preachers who go beyond the time limit expected for worship may be criticized for their lack of organization. Leaders who ignore the rhythms of their local communities are likely to be criticized for lack of attention to the world they supposedly serve.

> *While clocks and calendars can be relentless, liberation is still possible as you imagine a future belonging to God.*

Adding to the existing regularities of clock and calendar are the seasons of the church year. In some church settings this means only Christmas and Easter. In an increasing number of churches across the denominations, however, the rhythm of the church year can involve the whole community in celebrating Lent, Pentecost, Epiphany, and Transfiguration Sunday. With multiple age groups engaged in the community's memory and envisioning of the future, the energy generated through worship can expand almost endlessly. This time perspective in congregations can be liberating as well as constraining. While clocks and calendars can be relentless, liberation is still possible as you imagine a future belonging to God.

Writer Madeleine L'Engle affirms that while both *kairos* and *chronos* are necessary, *kairos* or sacred time is crucial for giving life meaning. She writes, "Kairos can sometimes enter, penetrate, break through chronos: the child at play, the painter at his easel, Serkin playing the *Appassionata*, are in kairos…. The bush, the burning bush, is in kairos, not any burning bush, but the very particular burning bush before which Moses removed his shoes" (*A Circle of Quiet*, Harper Collins edition, 1984, p. 245).

Freedom to preach is a double gift: experiencing both the regularity of *chronos* and the surprising encounter of *kairos*. Both are essential.

QUESTIONS FOR REFLECTION

Consider these questions for reflection and discussion. Raise other issues as they emerge in your group setting.

1. What were your first thoughts or images related to the title of this book?

2. What liberates or constrains you in your local community? In your denomination or tradition?

3. What is your current vision of preaching?

4. To what extent is your present practice or view of preaching governed by the clock? By the calendar?

5. What are the positive or negative associations for you of a "preaching pilgrimage?"

6. What would you say, today, if someone asked you, "what are you waiting for?"

Chapter 2:

Toward the North:
Breathing the Spirit

s I lived with the idea of a book called FREEDOM IN THE PULPIT, images of space and time became more and more important. I knew that spirituality was a deep concern for me as well as for other preachers I had met over the years. While it might seem obvious that a person working with the Bible and the Church would automatically feel a spiritual connection, I knew that such a connection did not always survive in Christian community. In developing my understanding of the need to think in *process* rather than *outcome* terms about preaching, I found myself moving toward the model of the compass, with its four directions or points, signifying four elements of preaching. It was only after months of working on this rough model that I remembered the Prayer for Centering from *The United Methodist Book of Worship*. It gave me words for the image I had been seeking. During the same month I found a visual representation of a Celtic knot from Scotland, and that became the graphic symbol for the book's cover, with its four points and its continuous interweaving of elements.

As you read the centering prayer, think of yourself in space, moving to the compass points as the prayer suggests.

A Prayer for Centering, in the Lakota Tradition

Paul reminds us that Christ is the center of creation,
    of our lives, and of the world.
We seek the wisdom of directions.
From each direction we return to the center
    reminded that Christ brings healing and salvation
    and by God's Spirit renews the face of the earth.
Let us be silent as we face our center point.

Let us face East.
From the East, the direction of the rising sun,
 we glean wisdom and knowledge
 through desert silences and humble service.
Enable us, O God, to be wise in our actions
 and in our use of the resources of the earth,
 sharing them in justice, partaking of them in gratitude.

Let us face South.
From the South come guidance and the beginning and end of life.
May we walk good paths, O God,
 living on the earth as sisters and brothers should,
 rejoicing in one another's blessing,
 sympathizing in one another's sorrows,
 and together look to you, seeking the new heaven and earth.

Let us face West.
From the West come purifying waters.
We pray that water might be pure and available to all,
and that we, too, may be purified
so that life may be sustained and nurtured
over the entire face of the earth.

Let us face North.
From the North come strong winds and gentle breezes.
May the air we breathe be purified
and may our lives feel that breath of the Spirit,
strengthening and encouraging us.

If we walked a path in each direction, the sacred paths would form a cross.
Returning to the center, we discover Christ,
 who calls us and challenges us.

—Adapted from a traditional Lakota prayer,
    The United Methodist Book of Worship, 1992, no. 470.

Though this prayer came to my awareness late in the process of writing the book, it seems to be a fitting gift of the Spirit. The four compass directions are potential guideposts for your own preaching pilgrimage. In my frame of reference, growing up as a European American living in the northeastern United States, I found it useful to begin with the compass direction to the North because of my early learnings about the North Pole, North Star, and North-facing landmarks such as Lake Erie. I realize that for people in the Southern hemisphere and for those in other cultural groups the North Pole may not be as fruitful for imagining a spiritual starting point. What is more important is that the prayer affirms all four compass directions and is centered on Jesus Christ as the center of creation, our lives, and the world.

You can consider the next compass direction, the East, in relation to the place where the sun rises, a new day begins, and preparing the Word for preaching can be located. The third compass point then becomes the South, where you will encounter and be encountered in the Body of Christ in worship. Joining the North and South Poles is a spiritual plumb line, linking the two poles through the earth's core. Finally, you can look toward the West compass direction as a place from which the preacher's growth can help in sustaining the community of preachers and leaders. At the smallest scale, you can look for those compass points as ways of orienting yourself during a particular day, week, or season in your preaching pilgrimage. At a larger scale, you can examine your movement toward or away from any of these compass directions and try to discern how you want to travel on the journey.

> *At the smallest scale, you can look for the compass points as ways of orienting yourself during a particular day, week, or season in your preaching pilgrimage.*

The compass is a spatial instrument that works if the traveler moves. Similarly, your own orientation to experiencing preaching can only become clearer and more useful if you are venturing out, taking steps and taking risks.

> From the North come strong winds and gentle breezes.
> May the air we breathe be purified
> and may our lives feel that breath of the Spirit,
>   strengthening and encouraging us.
>   (*The United Methodist Book of Worship*, no. 470)

When I was a youngster going to Girl Scout Camp in Ohio, we were taught that the most essential piece of hiking equipment was our compass. As long as we knew which way was north we could get back to the center of camp. If we lost our compasses, we could wander through acres of pine trees and not be able to tell which way was home.

Now that I live in Nashville, Tennessee, I lack the clearest landmark I grew up with — Lake Erie. Metropolitan Nashville does have a

> *Preaching cannot be done without a compass. You can only give directions home if you know the way yourself.*

much smaller lake within its boundaries—Radnor Lake Recreation Area. Because I am often unsure about which direction I am walking when going around the Radnor Lake hiking trails, I depend on directional signs to tell me which trail turns toward which other trail and which trail will lead me back to the parking area.

Preaching cannot be done without a compass. *You can only give directions home if you know the way yourself.* These days that knowledge can get jostled out of place by immediate tasks, worries, and an absence of a daily anchoring in spiritual disciplines. Simply being too busy can keep you from remembering who you are and where you are.

In the beginning of my attempts at preaching, my own life story was divorced from the task of the sermon. My sense of freedom came when I ceased to view the sermon as a laborious exercise in exegesis (existential bore-doom) and realized it as an expression of my own life journey as it intersected the biblical story. . . . I find that I make the greatest impact in my preaching when I am vulnerable enough to make available to the woundedness and joy of others what I have learned through an honest struggling and celebrating of my own woundedness and joy.

Lamar

There is strength in vulnerability. When the pastor is willing to share his/her own struggle along with the hope of the gospel, preaching becomes incarnational and inspires courage and hope for others seeking to be on the journey of faith.

David

A compass will not do you any good if you are running around too fast to read it! To change to another spatial metaphor, the congregational business of administration, report writing, fundraising, and conflict mediation can grow like bamboo shoots in a vegetable garden. When I moved to Eugene, Oregon, I thought that bamboo was an exotic and beautiful plant. Only later did I find out that bamboo could not be stopped. My neighbors became unwilling bamboo-growers, and I became unable to keep the bamboo from spreading. Paperwork and long meetings can spread in similar ways. You can get lost in the unwelcome growths and wonder what you intended to plant in the first place.

> **Preaching can become a job like any other, a task to be accomplished rather than a celebration to be shared.**

Recovering the Breath of the Spirit

It may seem unnecessary to say that a preacher's spiritual grounding in Jesus Christ is essential for joyful and authentic preaching. But preaching can become a job like any other, a task to be accomplished rather than a celebration to be shared. Evidence from hundreds of conversations with new and experienced pastors confirms that the spiritual formation of those who preach cannot be taken for granted or maintained sporadically.

Virginia Samuel Cetuk of Drew Theological School conducted research with incoming and graduating seminary students concerning their experiences of spirituality when they entered and later completed their seminary studies. Many felt their spiritual disciplines were solid and reliable, but within weeks of beginning school they were not continuing those spiritual disciplines. While engaging in intensive scholarly reading and test-taking, they were not experiencing God's daily presence. Many were leaving seminary with a strong sense of fatigue and bewilderment, and even cynicism (reported in Virginia Samuel Cetuk's forthcoming Abingdon book on spiritual formation and theological education).

Veteran United Methodist pastor Zan W. Holmes, Jr., has reported in his video in *Staying ALIVE in the Pulpit*, Series One, that in the midst of his long years as a pastor he suddenly realized that he was "mining the Bible for texts" rather than listening to the scriptures devotionally. After he stopped to realize that he had become a technician in the pulpit, he could begin again to listen to God, as a person with an authentic journey of his own. Success in preaching made him especially vulnerable. Being good at preaching tempted him toward pride in his own accomplishments instead of gratitude for the continuing challenge of preaching.

Pastor and writer Eugene Peterson describes two temptations that lead pastors to be pulled away from the essential task of being spiritual guides for congregations. One temptation is to become predominantly a manager-administrator, making the wheels turn and depending on efficiency rather than on prayer. The other is to evolve into a kind of local messiah, taking on all the pains and struggles of ministry oneself instead of enabling the congregation to develop in ministry. Either direction can bring rewards, but both lead away from the spiritual core of the local church (*Under the Unpredictable Plant*, Eerdmans, 1992).

How do you keep the main thing the main thing in local church ministry? How do you keep yourself connected to the compass point that represents your own North Pole? One answer is to find a way to be a spiritual learner and listener along with being a source of speaking and addressing problems. For people called into ministry the choice to serve is conscious and continuing. While choosing to serve, however, you can lose your own identity as a hungry child of a loving divine parent. *So the first part of this process of study and reflection focuses on your own spiritual journey.* The North Pole of your ongoing relationship to God in Christ is the compass direction that connects with everything else you do in ministry.

> **The North Pole of your ongoing relationship to God in Christ is the compass direction that connects everything else you do in ministry.**

Spiritual Leadership: Personal and Public

A pastor/preacher's decisions about how to deal with one's own journey, struggles, crises, and uncertainties are questions of spiritual discernment. Part of the

> *To preach a generic one-situation-fits-all sermon is to say that this moment, these people, and you as an individual are interchangeable parts. The Bible, however, does not portray the world or human beings as interchangeable.*

complexity of the preaching task is that preaching is both personal and public communication. You can avoid taking a stand when you proclaim the gospel, but by your very act of speaking you will be making theological choices about emphasis and values. To preach a generic one-situation-fits-all sermon is to say that this moment, these people, and you as an individual are interchangeable parts. The Bible, however, does not portray the world or human beings as mutually interchangeable. The parables offer concrete stories of believable people in understandable situations. The leaders in both the Hebrew Bible narratives and the New Testament gospel reveal themselves to be fallible. Most important, Christ is a personal savior, not an abstraction.

You cannot know what is going to provide access for others' memories, imaginations, and stories that will open them to the personal possibilities of the Jesus story. Ironically, one of the most reliable ways that people recognize the *universals* of human experience is through opening the doors into *one person's* consciousness, as the writer Frederick Buechner affirms. One communicator's openness can open doors for others because so many of us long to have our own story shared in another's reflections.

> My assumption is that the story of any one of us is in some measure the story of us all. For the reader, I suppose, it is like looking through someone else's photograph album. What holds you, if nothing else, is the possibility that somewhere among all those shots of people you never knew and places you never saw, you may come across something or someone you recognize. . . .On one of them you may even catch a glimpse of yourself . . . through which you glimpsed, however dimly and fleetingly, the sacredness of your own journey.
>
> *Listening to Your Life: Daily Meditations with Frederick Buechner,* compiled by George Connor. Harper/San Francisco, 1992, pp. 10-11.

Openness borne of pain is often the most powerful of all. A colleague told me recently that pastors in southern California, worn out by a year of earthquake, social rebellion, and intergroup conflicts, found themselves too tired for squabbles. They were thus able to listen to, lean on, and worship with each other with unusual grace. At times those problems you are most afraid will be damaging actually become the means for seeing each other with new eyes.

Grace Note from a Preacher's Pilgrimage

On October 19, 1994, Wednesday, at the Upper Room Chapel in Nashville, the words would not come. Not just the words I wanted to write, but all words. I was silenced.

I was intent on completing *Freedom in the Pulpit*, the book I had been wanting to write for half a dozen years. I had papers spread out across a large table in another upper room, a second floor office across the parking lot from my General Board of Discipleship office. I came to work early to get in some extra writing before chapel. I thought I might possibly meet the book deadline if everything worked out perfectly. But things were not working out that way.

I was worrying about my mother's recent biopsy for cancer. I was trying not to admit my fear that her present illness—coming after several surgeries, the amputation of a leg, and her continuing, relentless pain—might be more than I could handle as her primary adult contact and local support.

My colleague Roger offered the sermon and then invited prayers of intercession. I intended to say my mother's name—Claire Bate—but I could not speak. I found myself toppling over on my right side, next to Roger's wife Beverly, and unable to get up. Beverly and then Roger realized something was wrong and arranged a phone call for help. Within a few minutes two emergency medical technicians were wheeling a gurney into the middle of the chapel. I could see and hear them, but I could not speak and I could not move.

Then an unbelievable thing happened—an experience of simultaneous panic and peace. I knew my body was out of control. I had no idea where the loss of speech and movement had come from or how long it would last. I was profoundly frightened. But at the same moment I was aware of being cared for and sustained. I knew I was in some strange and amazing way safe.

Later in the hospital my ability to speak and walk began to return. By nightfall tests confirmed that there had been a clot or tear in the section of the left carotid artery controlling speech performance. Several days later I went home to recuperate. My brother arrived from Arizona to begin arranging for my mother's move to his city. My twelve year old daughter Joanna helped me around the house, and at the same time showed her own anxiety when I would get words like "helshe" or "yesterday/tomorrow" reversed. Both of us wanted to think that my mini-stroke was temporary and that it had no lasting results.

Six months after the T.I.A. (transitory ischemic attack) another test revealed that although I could speak relatively normally, the left carotid artery was still totally blocked. That sounded serious, even dangerous. But my doctor said surgery was not needed because the body had built other blood vessels to bring necessary blood into my brain. When I did not know it, I was healing.

I must have needed another kind of healing as well. While working to complete the book manuscript the second time around, I told several people who knew of my October experience that "it wouldn't be appropriate to put this in the book— it's private, and it won't read well." In truth, I was afraid to say that the experience might prove to other people that I was damaged, incomplete, vulnerable. Then one friend put his finger on the source of my mental blockage. "Well, when you preach you stand up and speak, and at that point you couldn't do either of them."

He was right. On October 19, 1994, I could not do what I treasured doing and thought I did well. Coming home from the hospital I wondered if I had also lost another capacity I treasure, playing the piano. When I went to my piano to see if I could still play my favorite piece, "Jesu, Joy of Man's Desiring," I realized that I was testing God. "God, are you going to let me be the person I thought I was? Are you telling me that I am not in charge of my life and my skills—that I can't take any of that for granted?" As I began to play "Jesu," I felt the answer coming. No. I am not "in charge" any more. I have experienced losing what I thought was my professional self, the one who stands and speaks. But the word grace has new meaning. There is a larger Yes. Life is a daily gift. Working on this book is simply one way to pass the gift along.

Barbara

A danger in the public role of the pastor or other spiritual leader is the temptation to seek safety in abstractions and theoretical ideas, so that people hearing the message —including you as the preacher—experience the word as a lecture, as information not related to the identity of the person speaking. Roger Ailes' book, You Are the Message (Doubleday Currency, 1988), confirms that tendency and

challenges speakers inside or outside the church to treat what they say ;
embodiment of their identity and personal vision rather than their role

When the invitational aspect of preaching
is effective, it is no more and no less than one
person inviting another or others into a mutual
hospitality borne of authentic personal experience. You cannot and need not invent that
hospitality, that encounter. You need only
make yourself available for breathing the Spirit
and looking in the direction of your own North
Pole. The Spirit of God will strengthen and
encourage us, in the words of the centering
prayer. As you allow yourself to subordinate
programs and organization to the centrality of being persons with other persons,
your identity as a leader will become more clear and your direction more coherent.

> *When the invitational aspect of preaching is effective, it is no more and no less than one person inviting another or others into a mutual hospitality borne of authentic personal experience.*

My 'home' pastor reminded me, before my first appointment, that the people in the pews wanted me to do well—as much as I wanted to preach well—so I enter the pulpit believing we are on a journey individually and together. Despite how carefully I craft my sermons, the Holy Spirit is really the one who carves the message. I can trust the Holy Spirit even when what I have to offer doesn't feel just right.

Margie

Nothing's a big deal unless I make a big deal out of it. There's only one thing worth making a big deal of and that is Jesus! I am determined to live by this the rest of my life.

Millie

In the previous chapter, "A Vision of Freedom," I outlined the elements or
phases of the primary task of the local congregation. These four processes need to
occur if the flow of God's love is to become realized and expanded through a faith
community and into the world. More than you may expect, the evangelical flow
of ministry rests on your own capacity as a preacher to be not only a leader in this
process but one of its receivers.

Preachers as Receivers of Ministry

Reached and received. Chances are that you have become a part of congregational ministry because of someone or something reaching out toward you and
making a difference in your life. It may be a series of experiences, or a particular
moment, or a long, quiet journey that continues to guide your life. Whatever the
sources, they have nourished and formed you. Your spiritual formation may have
begun decades ago, or only recently. What is important in any case is that you
know and remember your own pilgrimage. It will keep you from losing track of

your spiritual compass.

Several years ago I met a pastor who had come close to giving up the vocation of ordained ministry. He mentioned a number of personal and congregational struggles that had led him to think he was inadequate and ill-suited for the work he had originally chosen. When I asked what changed, he reported that there had been no bolt from the blue, but simply a chance to become part of a small group of colleagues. To his surprise he learned that his struggles were not unusual. Listening to his own story along with those of others he gradually realized that his call to serve God was more important to him than his imperfections. He began to imagine himself again as one of the Body of Christ.

When my wife almost died having our first child, I discovered that God wasn't with me in spite of my struggle. God was with me in the midst of the struggle we were facing! That has helped me many times in preaching on God's love in the midst of suffering.

Michael

Relating to God. Think of yourself as sitting in the first pew during worship, rather than seated behind the pulpit. People sitting on the first pew often get to church late and walk in uncomfortably aware that they are visible to others. But one benefit of this visibility is that they can see clearly and hear well. You are likely to pay attention when you are within a few feet of the pastor. That is precisely the position of the person who preaches—close to the worship event, able to listen acutely.

What are you to listen for? Having worked with adult learners in both public speaking and preaching classrooms, I think about the differences between the two. An obvious distinction is that you can expect to deal with any topic in a speech, whereas preaching has to do with God or with Christian topics. But that is not the essential point. The distinction of topic is far less important than the question of preaching's purpose and impact. You can give a speech about a religious topic such as denominational and nondenominational churches. You can include in it accurate and useful facts. The speech might be a helpful learning tool for a group of sociologists. If you hope to be ready to preach, however, you will need to be *formed* and *changed* within yourself so that in the process of preaching you encounter something from the Spirit of God and the world around you that was not available to you until then.

As a preacher I can be liberated from print, have penetrating eye contact, be at ease with my voice, and not necessarily be free in the pulpit. Freedom in the pulpit is a far deeper matter than the extent to which I have mastered performative skills. Rather, to be free in the pulpit is to know in my soul that I am infinitely loved, have received grace to salve my deepest wounds and pardon for all the pain I have dished out. To be emancipated for preaching is to have found the courage to unbar the door to the stranger within, both to make peace with my fears and to claim my unknown powers. Then I truly know gospel. I can be the person Christ is enabling me to be. I don't have to pretend to be anyone else. I'm free to preach the gospel.

Don

Nurtured in community and equipped for discipleship. Don's statement sheds light on the need for the preacher to continue in the process of becoming a disciple. If you are used to giving help to others, you may have been accustomed to *serving* more than *being served*. Is it possible for people who preach and lead worship to be formed and transformed as disciples themselves? It is not only possible but essential! Spiritual leaders as much as those in other human services need continuing connection with peers and fellow pilgrims. If you are a key part of other persons' support systems, you may need in particular peers and colleagues who will challenge you toward your full potential. In a peer situation you may have a chance to remove the "Helper-Fixer Hat" and be an individual disciple-in-process.

> *If you are a key part of other persons' support systems, you may need in particular peers and colleagues who will challenge you toward your full potential.*

Accountable discipleship takes effort to be fruitful. Roy Oswald, the author of *Clergy Support Systems* (Alban Institute, 1992), asks a series of questions designed to reveal how seriously you are looking for and finding community for yourself. He asks,

> Are you currently engaged with people [outside your immediate family] who...
> —Level with you?
> —Care enough to hold you accountable?
> —Let you be real?
> —Ask you difficult questions?
> —Enjoy you?
> —Give you a sense of your own worth and integrity?
> —Help you live with the pain of being different, alone, isolated?
> —Affirm that you are competent while allowing you to ask for help?
> —Call forth the best that is in you, evoking your gifts?
> (*Clergy Support Systems*, p.29)

Sent forth into the world as disciples. If you are a congregational leader, you are by definition in the business of change. Trying to bring growth in a community, trying to address major societal issues, or simply trying to remain sane in a demanding vocation—each can challenge your patience and your skills. At the same time you can be aware of yourself as a recipient of change. Every time a life begins or ends you are a witness of Creation. Every time you see people coming to new insight or renewing a relationship, you are in touch with the Body of Christ. By doing no more than hanging around a congregation, you can be continually sent forth into the world, if you pay attention to what is happening around you.

At the end of this century, when self-conscious God-talk is often problematic for skeptical observers, you can be incarnational without being inflammatory. A leader who is in God's presence as a person in the world can embody caring about the world and its maker. There is no single channel for God's working in you. You can nourish the creating Spirit in a number of ways. Allow yourself new opportunities—cooperative worship planning, alternative approaches to preaching or music, even recreational activities that call forth different talents and unexpected gifts in your surroundings. Can you go forth as one who waits for and celebrates the whole creation?

> **By doing no more than hanging around a congregation, you can be continually sent forth into the world, if you pay attention to what is happening around you.**

As you consider each of the four phases of the church's ministry as experiences that need to happen in you as well, you may feel some discomfort. You may think that these are a diversion from a central focus on effectiveness in preaching. Yet it is your capacity to see yourself as a *receiver of ministry*, as one who both cannot deliver and need not deliver all of God's grace, that will allow you to keep growing as a preacher and keep hearing what God will say in your life.

Daily Conversion

During my seminary studies in Chicago, I encountered Father Elias Chacour, a Melkite Orthodox priest from Galilee. He had been a child during the Zionist movement to establish the nation of Israel, and the members of his family were dislocated when their village was overtaken in that movement. His ministry over four decades has focused on fostering dialogue among Christians and Jews in a constantly conflicted nation. In his course on Christian Spirituality he influenced my life through the questions he challenged each student to ask. Each class session he would talk matter-of-factly about his need to continue his daily conversion into faith. Each time we met he would look directly at students and ask, "On whose face do you see the face of God?" One result of studying with Father Chacour was a changed perspective about the difference between public and personal communication. Father Chacour's personal history was consistently united with his ministry. His words were integral—whole and of a piece—and thus carried integrity. In a similar sense, *preaching asks the person in the pulpit to be whole and of a piece when speaking with others.* Private or privileged knowledge is not necessary to convey that you have been there in a particular life struggle. Others will seek to know

> **Others will seek to know you as a person walking through life, not as a commentator lecturing about life.**

you as a person walking through life, not as a commentator lecturing about life.

Part of our need to experience conversion into the preaching task comes from the temptations toward expertise and adulation. Believing that you are talented can make you crazy with the desire to win a faster race, write a more famous book, lead a larger church. The lack of a belief that you are highly expert at your craft can also be debilitating. Some pastors of smaller sized congregations suffer from lowered self-esteem and lowered hopes. A culture that gives grades to everything from physical education in school to outsized zucchinis at state fairs conveys to large numbers of people that winning is what counts. Cutting loose from this cultural mania for competition and prizewinning is not easy, but it is clearly a scriptural mandate.

The preaching and teaching of Jesus, Paul, Peter, Mary Magdalene, and other bringers of God's good news had impact but not immediate rewards. Looking further back in time, the need for continuing work is evidenced by the Hebrew Bible's many stories of God's second, third, and myriad chances given to fallible human beings. You may never know exactly

> **You may never know exactly when the words spoken in worship will become the Word of life for another person.**

when the words spoken in worship will become the Word of life for another person. As you continue to practice the spiritual disciplines of prayer, Scripture reading, worship, and covenantal dialogue, however, you will find the Spirit of God breathing into and through your days.

QUESTIONS FOR REFLECTION

Consider these questions for reflection and discussion. Raise other issues as they emerge in your group setting.

1. What images or experiences does the phrase "breathing the Spirit" bring to you?

2. When are you most confident of God's presence? When do you "see the face of God" and find God reaching and receiving you? What disciplines aid you in this process?

3. What happens to you when you experience God as silent or absent?

4. What kind of community is available to nurture and challenge you?

   • Who are your Mary, Susanna, and Joanna, providing resources for your journey?

   • Who is your truthtelling prophet Nathan?

   • Who calls you out of the tomb, when you would stay enshrouded in the dark?

5. What aspects of spiritual leadership lead you to be anxious, uncomfortable, or uncertain? What do you do in those situations?

6. Describe what you characterize as your 'call to preach,' your vocation toward preaching and worship leadership.

Chapter 3:
Toward the East:
Preparing the Word

From the East, the direction of the rising sun,
    we glean wisdom and knowledge
    through desert silences and humble service.
Enable us, O God, to be wise in our actions
    and in our use of the resources of the earth,
    sharing them in justice, partaking of them in gratitude.
             (*The United Methodist Book of Worship*, no. 470)

Several mornings a week I swim laps in the YMCA pool near my home. For three years I have used the indoor pool, where I am familiar with its length and can judge my distance during the backstroke by looking up at the sky-lights. This past summer the Y opened its outdoor pool and its indoor pool was briefly closed for repairs. So I went outdoors to do my mixture of breaststroke, crawl, and backstroke. Suddenly I realized that I couldn't tell where I was during the backstroke. I veered to one side, nearly into the path of another swimmer. Losing my orientation point, I lost my usual ability to swim in a straight direction.

My swimming experience reminded me of the double nature of preaching. As a preacher you are given a gift of phenomenal freedom and at the same time a responsibility for structure and discipline. The Holy Spirit does not represent an alternative to Scripture and community. The opposite is true. Scriptural history and witness can guide you away from a temporary myopia. Living along with other Christian pilgrims can keep you honest as you go eye to eye with a congregation of real people.

Freedom and Discipline: The First Time and the Next Time

The East is the fitting compass point for this part of the preaching pilgrimage. The East is, in nature and in many cultures, a symbol of beginnings. Whether you are beginning to imagine preaching for the first time or looking at a particular gospel passage for the twentieth time, this moment can become new. The East is literally the source of the new day and the rising of the sun, "God's re-creation of the new day" according to the popular contemporary song-hymn, "Morning Has Broken." I suggest the Eastern marker of the preaching compass as the location for preparing to preach—as a gift and as a discipline. For those of us who are most alert in the morning, the idea of developing and forming ideas fits well with the image of moving from dawn into the morning. But even people who do not wake up with the dawn sometimes find themselves able to focus on essential ideas or tasks when they are away from the busy-ness of schedules later in the day.

Jesus' preaching and teaching provide us with images, though not precise models, for contemporary preaching. The core of the gospel message is visual and visionary. You are asked to commit yourself to a wider vision, seeing people as they are and as they can be. In doing this you move naturally beyond your own success as a communicator. So the second part, not the first part, of the preacher's pilgrimage is preparation. You can only prepare for a preaching event with integrity after you have been on the spiritual journey yourself. The journey is not just a series of separate events, but an ongoing experience that you can separate only arbitrarily into frozen frames.

> **You can only prepare for a preaching event with integrity after you have been on the spiritual journey yourself.**

A major issue for navigating in this part of the journey is how to experience a mix of newness and familiarity. Routine alone deadens; novelty alone becomes chaotic. A goal worth seeking is a mix of the two—openness to the Spirit and to new learning, and simultaneously an order or routine sufficient to avoid disaster.

One physical discipline that works for some preachers is to go away from the place you typically prepare to preach—by driving, standing in the shower, walking around the block, gardening, cooking, or some other physical activity that releases the mind while involving the body in its own operations.

> **The important thing is not to have a single way of preaching for all time, but to develop patterns that honor the gospel and respect the voice of yourself as a spiritual guide and communicator.**

How can you "prepare" to preach? The important thing is not to have a single way of preaching for all time, but to develop patterns that honor the gospel and respect the voice of yourself as a spiritual guide and communicator. Preachers who are not in the pulpit every week sometimes say it is difficult to gear themselves for the full process of preaching. Other infrequent preachers describe their experiences as comparable to riding a bicycle after years away. You know that your body once knew the moves, but the first few minutes can leave you feeling unsteady.

Rhetoric from Ancient and Modern Teachers

The teacher Aristotle had some of the best ideas from any age in dealing with how to prepare a message and make it persuasive for others. Aristotle's *Rhetoric* (translated by Lane Cooper, 1960) stated the belief that a person must discover the available means of persuasion in each particular case. That idea is compatible with Jesus' preaching and teaching in the New Testament. Know the people around you, know what they care about, and be ready to make their concerns visible and meaningful through what you say.

Aristotle's students recorded five essential areas or aspects of rhetoric, paraphrased here for the purpose of showing their relatedness to preaching in worship:
- **Invention**—creativity—generating ideas with the help of the Spirit
- **Organization**—arranging the parts—developing movement and momentum within and beyond the moment of preaching
- **Language**—words—phrases, images, rhythms
- **Memory**—continuity and connection with message and receivers
- **Delivery**—nonverbal, vocal, physical message elements—presence.

Aristotle was not particularly interested in religious communication. His goal was to train brilliant students for political and legal discourse. Aristotle's insights are relevant today, however, because preaching is rhetorical; it seeks change. *When you preach you are using human communication techniques to accomplish change.*

In this segment of the book, "Preparing the Word," the focus is particularly on what Aristotle called *invention, organization,* and *language style.* The next segment will look at the elements of *memory* and *delivery* as essential for "Encountering the Body of Christ" in worship. As throughout this book, the labels are somewhat arbitrary. The preaching pilgrimage does not have tight, absolute boundaries.

Twentieth century writers on rhetoric have built on Aristotle's framework for thinking about the ways to communicate for change and transformation. Several decades ago, Kenneth Burke recognized that religious as well as other messages bring people into at least temporary unity with one another through *mutual identification*—the joining of interests and awareness among persons in a communication situation (*A Grammar of Motives,* Harper and Row, 1950). This identification can be strategic and intentional on the part of a persuader; but in Christian community it is more than a strategy. Rhetorical identification meets our human longing to connect with others.

During this decade, writer Robin Meyers has affirmed that preaching is not only a matter of persuading other persons through intentional communication, but also an experience of *self-persuasion* in which the preacher is the first hearer of his or her own message, and thus

> **The preacher is the first hearer of his or her own message, and thus someone likely to be changed in the process of preaching.**

someone likely to be changed in the process of preaching (*With Ears to Hear: Preaching as Self-Persuasion*, Pilgrim Press, 1993). When it is authentic self-persuasion, preaching influences the one who speaks as much as it does the ones who receive the persuasive message. This does not mean that you are simply preaching for yourself, but it does mean that you belong in worship as a *participating* member of the Body of Christ.

Engaging the Three Worlds in Preaching

Behind Aristotle's original notion of rhetorical invention is the concern for where ideas and experiences originate. In terms of preparing to preach, what focuses your attention? What seems worthwhile to speak about with others in worship? A modern answer to these questions is offered by *the three worlds in preaching*. Whatever your training or routine for preparing to preach, you need to include three worlds or domains in worship—the world of Scripture, the world of the community, and your own domain, the world of the preacher. (These ideas have been summarized earlier in Michael Williams' *Preaching Pilgrims: An Ecumenical Guide to Excellence in Preaching*, Discipleship Resources, 1987.)

- The first of the three preaching life-worlds, the world of *the Scriptures*, is essential, for there is no Christian preaching that is not biblical preaching.

THE THREE WORLDS IN PREACHING

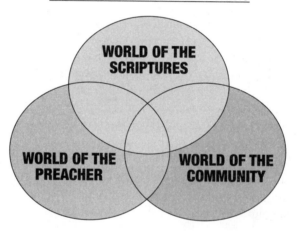

- In the second domain, preaching necessarily comes from and into a corporate, gathered *community*—including people in your congregation and other communities that you recognize as part of the Body of Christ.
- In the third domain, the world of *the preacher* involves the one who proclaims the gospel as a pilgrim, a leader, and a person of integrity.

As you prepare to preach, each of these worlds or realms of experience needs to be taken into account as you listen to and form a message to be shared in worship. You can engage your imagination as well as your training in gathering material in the three domains. This is essential work—generating material in light of God's creating Spirit.

The questions below will give you guidance about where and how to look for appropriate materials in the three worlds.

Entering the World of Scripture: Considering a Biblical Text

- What are your reactions to this text?
- What is your most vivid impression/feeling on reading it this time?
- What (if anything) bothers or puzzles you about it, including strangeness or overfamiliarity?
- What do you know about its original context(s)?
- What kind of material predominates: a story, a sensory image, a truth claim?
- If the Scripture is based in story, what do you see or hear? What do the people in the story see, hear, or feel?
- How is this passage reinforced or called into question by other biblical materials?

Entering the World of the Community

- Describe the congregation in demographic terms—age, gender and racial-ethnic mix, socioeconomic situation, geographic location.
- What does your congregation see as its mission?
- What are the markers, positive or negative, of spirituality in this community?
- How do you characterize the formal and informal leaders in your congregation? How are they chosen or sustained? Do you preach to/for them?
- How does your local congregation relate to its surroundings—to other churches, to other social groups, other regions, the nation, the world?
- What are the favorite stories of your congregation? Do they center in the past, the present, an immediate future, an everlasting future?

Entering Your World as a Preacher

- What section of the Bible appeals to you most? Why?
- How do the biblical texts for this week relate to your current spiritual life?
- Does an event, experience, or memory connect you to a particular passage?
- Is there comfort or pain attached to this passage?
- What seems inappropriate to say but truthful to your experience?
- What do you wish you could hear if you were in the pew next Sunday?

The questions above can be a helpful way to walk into and listen to a biblical text. Or, you can visualize the three worlds and, quite literally, play with them. Use the space on page 47 to try the visual and graphic process suggested below.

1. Make three circles on a page—Scripture, Community, Preacher.
2. Place inside each of them a word, picture, or other symbol of something that seems important from your own reflection as you consider your next time to preach.
3. As you begin to imagine the preaching moment, think about which circle you would find most comfortable entering first. How could you move from

one circle to another? Do you see any link or links between them? Live with the question for a while.

4. Where is the "fun" in this experience thus far? What gathers or blocks your energy as you are engaging in this process?
5. How might other people identify with you—see or hear along with you?
6. "So what?" What is emerging here that can nurture/challenge/equip the listeners to make the message their own, complete it, and act it out in the world?

You may or may not find these two sets of questions useful. Before you decide whether to adopt or reject either of them, consider the following statement, recounting the tendency of thinking adults to encounter "vicious circles."

> The creative processes of free play and concentrated practice can be derailed. They can go spinning off into addiction or procrastination, into obsession or obstruction, leaving us, outside our own natural flow of activity, in states of confusion and self-doubt. . . .Practice is the reciprocal of addiction. Practice is an ever-fresh, challenging flow of work and play in which we continually test and demolish our own delusions; therefore it is sometimes painful. . . . The ego wants to be right, but in the dynamics of life and art we are never right, we are always changing and cycling.
>
> Stephen Nachmanovitch, *Free Play: The Power of Improvisation in Life and the Arts*, Jeremy Tarcher, 1990, pp. 126-129.

If you can enjoy the creative flow of the Spirit, you may be able to move away from a vicious circle and toward the kind of experience Rick describes below.

There is an emotional/physiological rush to preaching—but I also enjoy the challenge, academic and creative, of making the Scripture relate to life.

Rick

WORSHEET FOR ENGAGING
THE THREE WORLD IN PREACHING

You can copy these circles as many times as you wish for future sermon preparation. They can serve as a process for letting the Spirit and the Word "play" along with you as you prepare to preach.

**WORLD OF THE
SCRIPTURES**

**WORLD OF THE
COMMUNITY**

**WORLD OF THE
PREACHER**

Listening and Receiving

Your options for discovering material for preaching are many. First among them is the need to listen faithfully, keeping yourself from pushing toward a final message until you have had a chance to hear the word from more than one angle. There are several ways to "hear" the Scriptures:

- You can examine several versions of the same passage.
- You can take other than the traditional roles of characters in biblical narratives (Eli rather than Samuel, the Pharaoh instead of the Israelites, Ananias and Sapphira instead of Peter).
- You can say the passage to yourself in colloquial speech.
- You can walk toward the past situation from the perspective of the present (the Emmaus pilgrims as rock music fans, or Mary as a teenage welfare mother).

The world of community, including your local congregation, provides ready and natural sources for listening to the situations, struggles, and hopes of the people around you. Your job is not to search for the failings of the parishioners and wave them about. Nor is it simply to say what everyone has heard before and no one finds current or crucial. The point in this creation/invention process is to lead yourself toward hearing and recognizing the Word's availability and relevance in the most natural ways you find possible.

> *Your job is not to search for the failings of the parishioners and wave them about. Nor is it simply to say what everyone has heard before and no one finds current or crucial.*

The Scriptures and the Common Lectionary

Increasing numbers of pastors choose sermon texts based on the Revised Common Lectionary of 1992 (available, among other places, in pages 227-237 of *The United Methodist Book of Worship*, United Methodist Publishing House, 1992). This lectionary includes a psalm, an epistle, a passage from the Hebrew Bible and a passage from one of the four gospels. Especially if you are a relatively new preacher, the lectionary can help increase the range of biblical materials your congregation will encounter over time. The passages often connect in theme or language, and they follow the pattern of the Christian year for each of three years. Advantages of the lectionary include:

- continuity across churches and often across denominations, allowing for study by ecumenical groups of pastors,
- the availability of liturgical, musical, and exegetical materials related to the lectionary, and
- the protection of the preacher from self-imposed limits of habit or personal interest that lead to repetition of the same themes.

The lectionary has limitations, however. It sometimes:

- excludes whole sections of the Bible,
- cuts short narratives, and
- avoids the complex or difficult segments of selected passages.

As Eugene Lowry has reported, "the lectionary loves the happy, the positive, and the closed" (*Staying ALIVE in the Pulpit*, Series Two, Discipleship Resources, 1995). Even with these limitations, the lectionary has the capacity to challenge you as a preacher. Below are two reports of pastors whose lectionary experiences forced them to confront biblical ideas that opened up a wider faith encounter.

My brother ran away from home several times. I still recall the pain and anger at my brother for causing my parents such grief and worry. Whenever the lectionary included the Prodigal Son I frequently chose the Old Testament or Epistle lesson... I finally decided to wrestle with the text. Not surprisingly, I easily identified with the older son in the story. The sermon that resulted was not terribly eloquent or neatly crafted. It was agonizing, terrifying. But mostly, it was a gift from God. The jealousies many of us have felt as God bestows on others the grace we seek for ourselves was confronted. God's grace flowed. The sermon I had long avoided became a blessed healing for many who heard and for the one who dared to preach.

Marian

Soon after the failure of my first marriage, the divorce passage came up in the gospel lectionary. I was almost in despair. I felt so unworthy to preach. I struggled with this in prayer and the thought came: "Who is worthy?" I came to the realization that it is only by grace that we preach—or hear, for that matter. No one can claim to be worthy. My sermon concentrated on the healing and forgiving grace available to those who have been broken and wounded by personal failures and tragedies—particularly by divorce. There continue to be more requests for copies of that sermon than any other I have preached.

Richard

Wrestling with a biblical text can leave a preacher limping, as did Jacob. At the same time the seeming unworthiness of the one who speaks is a symbol of the God who comes to be with us in our most earthly, incomplete, and thereby accessible selves.

Using Preaching Resources

Writings intended to help preachers prepare for the pulpit have proliferated during the past two decades. Lectionary study books, periodicals, interpretive guides, and collections of complete sermons are available if you have the funds to purchase or subscribe to them. One recent workshop focused entirely on the various printed resources available for preaching preparation.

What about all this material? There are huge differences among the kinds of resources currently in the religious marketplace. Some of them may open you to new ways of seeing, hearing, and feeling the truth of God's Word. Others, by the very nature of their prepackaging of biblical themes and conclusions, can restrict you from following your own path or experiencing biblical passages in ways that have power and worth in your own context.

One implication of this double truth is that you need to begin with your own encounter with biblical texts, not with commentaries and interpreters. Whatever

> **You need to _begin_ with your own encounter with biblical texts, not with commentaries and interpreters.**

their academic or pastoral credentials, commentators cannot bring together the three worlds essential to preaching—not only the scriptural world, but also the world of the congregation and community, and the world of the preacher himself or herself.

There is no single correct way to prepare for preaching in worship. The ideas in this segment have come from working with beginning and more experienced preachers, and from observing my own process of preparing for worship. The predominant issue I encounter is the issue of how to *become free to hear the Word*, to bring it in a coherent and empowering way to other people.

> *I struggle with what could be called "preacher's block." Sometimes it is very hard for me to let the text tell me what it should and needs to communicate to me. I have found two helpful hints. First, naming the feelings I experience from hearing the story of the text can unlock the power of the text. Second, I will focus upon a key word from the text itself or implied from the text. Letting my imagination play with this key word can release the direction and meaning of the text for me.*
>
> *Ben*

Freedom in preparing to preach most certainly does not mean freedom from having to work at it. I wince when I hear about a preacher who opens a Bible during Sunday worship, speaks off the cuff for several minutes, and then announces to those listening that they will be reached by the Word if they are simply open to the Holy Spirit. This is not freedom; it is irresponsibility. It leaves the listeners increasingly skeptical about the preacher's motives and capabilities. Especially when a pastor has been ordained to Word and Sacrament, the skepticism of listeners can contribute to a crumbling of trust between pastors and laypersons within a community. Each person who preaches owes all who listen our God-created selves at our best. You are encouraged to be like the lilies of the field—not in order to be lazy, but in order to be free of anxious concerns that may keep you from doing the task you are called to do.

> **Each person who preaches owes all who listen our God-created selves at our best.**

Forming and Shaping

Many different lists are available to help you organize speeches and sermons. Lists can be useful if you have a single idea and lack a sense of how to bring it to life over a period of time. The more important issue in organization, however, does not involve randomly or routinely picking a pattern. It is discovering how the pattern you choose to form and shape a message builds into a unified whole, bringing transformation in you and in those with whom you preach and lead worship.

> Those who order ideas and whose task therefore is to organize will find their sermon form to be a structure. Those who order experience and whose task therefore is to shape will find their sermon form to be a process.
> Eugene Lowry, *Doing Time in the Pulpit: The Relationship Between Narrative and Preaching*, Abingdon, 1985, p. 17.

> Creating rather than selecting a form involves delaying that which is the concern of every preacher, acquiring a structure or outline for the sermon. More exactly, it involves subordinating the quest for a form to another interest, one more vital to lively and effective preaching. Instead of asking, What is a good outline I can use for this message? one asks, What is the major communicative burden of this sermon? In other words, What has to be done in order to get this message heard?
> Fred B. Craddock, *Preaching*, Abingdon, 1985, p. 182.

Any pattern or arrangement that lets you connect materials you have already found fruitful can be helpful. A caution is in order: *a single pattern can be hypnotic if you use it as a consistent routine or crutch.* Keep your options open as you listen and look for the unity emerging within the preaching process as it develops. The Spirit of God can enable your creativity when you least expect it.

Public messages from inside or outside the pulpit tend to take forms that parallel familiar

> **Keep your options open as you listen and look for the unity emerging within the preaching process as it develops. The Spirit of God can enable your creativity when you least expect it.**

forms of human perception and memory. Homiletics teacher David Schlafer has described three ways of organizing material—image, narrative, and argument—that appear in daily life as well as in Scripture (*Surviving the Sermon: A Guide to Preaching for Those Who Have to Listen*, Cowley, 1992). Considering these patterns can help you to develop coherent messages from the pulpit. The three strategies are shown below.

IMAGE	NARRATIVE	ARGUMENT
sensory materials	story of events in sequence	claims based on reasoning
sheep; mustard seed; oil for anointing	The father rushes to meet his returning younger son	Jesus said, "I am the way, the truth, and the life."
Models: specific Scriptural objects or persons	Models: birth story; parable	Models: Ten Commandments; Beatitudes

Any of the three strategies can be the basis for structuring a message. As you plan your preaching for a given worship event, you may not know at the outset of your planning process which of the three will be most appropriate as a response to that biblical text. You may decide to follow the form of the original message, to use another aspect of the original. For example, a focus on the image of "home" in the prodigal son parable, or the argument claim that "each of us has gone away from home," may emerge to fit better in the service as a whole. Because worshipers can be responsive to varying kinds of verbal material, your preaching needs to include image, argument, and narrative in some way because all three are natural elements of communication and thought. One of the three should predominate so that the focus and movement of the preaching will remain clear to you and your listeners.

The Language of Experience

When new preachers or lay speakers get ready to lead children's sermons, the dangers of adult-oriented words become visible. Children coming forward in worship want to please the adult in charge; the adult leader tries to say something adults consider important enough to be worth saying. The problem is that adults are often accustomed to concept nouns such as "grace" and "salvation" and young children are more accustomed to action or object words such as "baseball" and "lunch" and "running down the street." Trying to link the two kinds of language—concept language and experience language—is the business not only of children's messages but of preaching with adults as well.

God gives us all kinds of wonderful places to play. But we turn them into hard work—and that is often what happens with preaching!

Deborah

Preaching is an appropriate place to bring together a concept or idea and an experience. Listeners can respond to a mixture of the general and the specific, the word-based concept and the image grounded in the senses (especially the visual sense). Linking these two kinds of language lets you respond to people who resonate to conceptual material, as well as to people who connect best with specific sensory images.

> *While Scripture is the primary source for my preaching, I use materials found in daily life. . . . I once discovered a tiny brilliant red mushroom beneath a huge beech tree. The mushroom was within a cavity filled with decaying wood. Not too long ago, I saw an elderly friend asleep in her wheelchair at the nursing home. In her lap, held between her thumb and fingers was a letter from a grandson. . . . We should not overlook the little things of daily life.*
>
> *Donald*

Preparing for preaching involves *an active receptivity* to what is around you. Be ready to engage with what God brings into your awareness rather than expecting that you will be given the perfect language through long and difficult study. The more education you have had, the harder this step can become. You can grit your teeth in the effort to control or take charge of what you read, hear, and see around you. Students of religion and philosophy often become accustomed to writing papers centered on concept language. People in the pews, and preachers themselves when they are acting as parents, neighbors, customers, or friends, use the language of image and story much more often than strings of concepts.

As mentioned earlier in the book, the essential difference in preaching is between data and human beings, *information* and *formation*. As I suggested in chapter two, lectures can inform, but *only in Christian community are people formed and transformed into disciples*. As one colleague put it, chasing the rabbits of your imagination can be a powerful way to encounter the Spirit in a community.

> If the primary preaching task of the pastor is the conversion of lives, the primary teaching task is the conversion of language. I haven't quit using the languages of information and motivation, nor will I. Competency in all languages is necessary in this life of faith that draws all levels of existence into the service and glory of God. But I have determined that the language in which I must be most practiced and for which I have a primary responsibility for teaching proficiency in others is Language I, the language of relationship, the language of prayer—to get as much language as possible into the speech of love and response and intimacy.
>
> Eugene H. Peterson, *The Contemplative Pastor: Returning to the Art of Spiritual Direction*, Eerdmans, 1989, pp. 93-94.

The need to work at your language for preaching is not a new phenomenon. The Bible is full of images and metaphors, and Jesus' preaching was largely in parables couched in everyday, concrete descriptions and narratives. Yet some of the most difficult aspects of language are those that seem most trivial—the pronouns, for example. Some of the smallest words in the English language carry some of the heaviest freight in terms of human relationships. These are the personal pronouns. For most of the twentieth century, preaching students and practicing preachers were taught not to use first person pronouns, particularly not the pronoun "I." The business of the preacher was to convey the word of God to the faith community, not to reveal personal concerns. But in the past two decades the understanding of the preacher as a person has evolved, both in teaching settings and in local churches. Today it can be a problem for people in worship when the person preaching never says "I" to the congregation. People listening to a preacher ask themselves, who is this person, and how does she or he view me and others around me?

Consider the differing ways that four pronouns can be used or abused in preaching.

- **"It"** is a term for concepts; it is an academic word, a word of analysis, a left-brained word. It can be a way to avoid acknowledging or affirming relationships at a personal level.

- **"We"** is a slippery pronoun. It can build or affirm community, as in cases where the leader's statement "we gather together" helps remind those present of their commitment to struggle amid division or conflict. But the word "we" can also be used to judge, setting a preacher above and apart from the community while appearing to connect the two. For example, a pastor's statement that "we have been slow in making our financial pledges this year" is likely to be received as referring to the church members rather than to the pastor, though it curves back toward the speaker as an implied complaint.

- **"You"** also has more than one possible tone. It can be used to attack, to label, or to confront others, whether out of caring or superiority. Take for example the prophet Nathan's simple yet damning words to King David: "You are the man!"(2 Samuel 12:7, NRSV) The word *you* can also be a word of encounter, of reaching out toward other persons in the spirit of dialogue.

- **"I"** has the potential to carry a preaching event into autobiography or self-aggrandizement for the preacher. On the other hand, it can also convey an honest pilgrimage on the part of the one who speaks, recognizing that he or she is a member of the community as well as a leader. Richard Thulin's book *The "I" of the Sermon* (Fortress, 1989) describes four helpful ways for you to discern whether your choices of "I" language are faithful to your purpose as you preach. Ranging from the least to the most involving of the preacher's self, the types of I-messages in first-person stories are:

"I" MESSAGES IN PREACHING

ILLUSTRATION	Little detail, and focus on general truths
REMINISCENCE	More detail, based on memory and thoughts of the preacher
CONFESSION	Example growing out of preacher's feelings relating to God
SELF-PORTRAYAL	Detailed account of preacher as person relating to God and the world, and as a witness in community

Whatever your current pattern or preference, the ultimate issue is not which pronoun or which form of story is the best. The point of knowing these options is to help you discern how your personal experience can help build Christian community.

QUESTIONS FOR REFLECTION

Reflect on these questions related to your experience of "Preparing the Word."

1. When you are getting ready to preach, what are your first thoughts, feelings, actions? How consistent or changeable is that pattern?

2. Of the life worlds of Scripture, community, and preacher, which is for you the most natural starting place? Which is least likely or least comfortable?

3. Where do you see yourself as most or least creative in generating a message?

4. What do you do to foster your creativity or imagination?

5. What are the signs for you that your current preaching preparation process is going well? What are your concerns about it?

6. What is your most frequent pattern for preaching—image, narrative, or argument? Your least frequent pattern?

7. What is your 'favorite' pronoun for preaching? Compare your response with that of someone whose preaching you enjoy.

CHAPTER 4:
TOWARD THE SOUTH:
ENCOUNTERING THE BODY OF CHRIST

Navigating the third compass point in the preaching pilgrimage is a matter of *experiencing worship*, as leader, participant, celebrating guest, and person transformed by the presence of God. The centering prayer provides images of this encounter.

> From the South come guidance and the beginning and end of life.
> May we walk good paths, O God,
>> living on the earth as sisters and brothers should,
>> rejoicing in one another's blessing,
>> sympathizing in one another's sorrows,
>> and together look to you, seeking the new heaven and earth.
>> (*The United Methodist Book of Worship*, no. 470)

How you imagine, plan, and conduct yourself in relation to the worship service is a spiritual matter as much as it is a matter of technique and control. Becoming a worshiper can be difficult for the pastor or other leader in charge of worship. It can also mean the difference between an encounter of the Spirit and a routine.

The key elements in this third compass direction are:

- involvement and honoring of the senses
- recognizing the power of gender and culture
- fostering the drama and momentum of worship
- hospitality and use of the imagination
- involving the congregation in the plumbline for worship.

Rueben Job, a longtime spiritual guide in The United Methodist Church, was kept out of school for a year during his childhood in North Dakota because of rheumatic fever. For the months in which he was too weak to go to school, his mother would begin each morning by placing him in the two-foot-wide windowsill of their family's earthen house. He sat in the sunlight of that South-facing window all day. As he describes the experience, he was fed by the Southern light every day. Eventually he became strong enough to leave the house and go to school. He says that this early experience of being warmed by his mother's care and the daily sunlight has affected him throughout his life.

Whatever region you live in, you are affected by the direction and the intensity of the sun's rays. In the mountains of northern New Mexico, for example, there can be a thirty degree difference in temperature between being beneath a tree and out in the open during a summer afternoon. That can mean the difference between heat exhaustion and comfort sufficient for conversation. The presence of the preacher can represent similarly the power of warmth and intense connection, a source of nourishment in and through the community. Your willingness to absorb and reflect the rays of the lives and concerns of other people generates energy that can flow from a service of worship into the lives of those who have worshiped together.

> **Your willingness to absorb and reflect the rays of the lives and concerns of other people generates energy that can flow from a service of worship into the lives of those who have worshiped together.**

The Senses in Worship

Worship is a form of communication that involves persons, time, space, and sound. The human senses affect the results because human beings are central to the experience. We humans act and respond to the worship experience through multiple sensory organs. These actions are complex and important to effective preaching and worship.

In some respects, worship is the most formal of human encounters. It is a ritual, occurring in a myriad of forms, places, and times. It is incarnational, making visible that God is with us in bodily form. As a spiritual leader you may be able to avoid the secular culture's preoccupation with physical appearance, but you cannot ignore the importance people give to the *perceptions* of authenticity and integrity. The fact that dishonesty is widespread in many public situations makes the question of authenticity loom large. People *decide* whose voice they will listen to in the church. They look for reliable rituals and spiritual guides to join them in those rituals. Robert Fulghum makes the point with elegant simplicity in a recent book.

> To be human is to be religious.
> To be religious is to be mindful.
> To be mindful is to pay attention.
> To pay attention is to sanctify existence.
> Rituals are one way in which attention is paid.
> Rituals arise from the stages and ages of life.
> Rituals transform the ordinary into the holy.
> Rituals may be public, private, or secret.
> Rituals may be spontaneous or arranged.
> Rituals are in constant evolution and reformation.
> Rituals create sacred time.
> Sacred time is the dwelling place of the Eternal.
> Haste and ambition are the adversaries of sacred time.
> Is this so?
>
> Robert Fulghum, *From Beginning to End: The Rituals of Our Lives.*
> Villard Books, 1995, p. 20.

How do people decide what rituals will be meaningful for them, and whose voices in leadership will influence them in those rituals? Nonverbal cues—the domain Aristotle referred to as *delivery*—are essential to those decisions. *Nonverbal aspects of your communication in worship are often believed and remembered more than the ideas in your sermons.* The verbal and the nonverbal are intertwined, intentionally.

In videotaping the preaching of pastors or seminary students, I have always made sure to stop the tape and rewind it to review a moment when the preacher's language and physical behaviors seem most clear and compatible with each other. Typically this is a time when the preacher is most committed to the words being said and least nervous about saying something clever to the congregation. Seeing and hearing the Word in action can help the preacher recognize and remember his or her distinctive voice for preaching.

> Authentic and passionate conversation is contagious. The preacher's level of intensity affects the level of listening and raises the stakes for everyone concerned. It is no accident that when a musical virtuoso performs, the level of music appreciation in the audience rises correspondingly. . . . Preaching as self-persuasion is no less a performance of the biblical score. Rhythms and crescendos exist in language as surely as in music. Melody lines and refrains, serving as they do to both unfold and remind, can be powerfully adapted to preaching. . . And what makes jazz work holds a lesson for the pulpit: it can never be the same way twice. But the test of good music is that it gets under your skin. It is an irresistible intruder, and you catch yourself humming the tune long after the performance is over.
>
> Robin R. Meyers, *With Ears to Hear: Preaching as Self-Persuasion*, Pilgrim Press, 1993, pp. 108-109.

presence as a preacher is a unified whole, not a list of anatomical
[...]t whole there are several major nonverbal elements that can
[...] your preaching. They include:

- direct eye contact toward the worshipers, looking to the faces of the individuals present rather than toward the ceiling, wall, or manuscript;
- a clear, audible, and conversational voice, with variety, emphasis, and pauses;
- body movements that fit your words and suggest comfort and confidence in the message;
- the appropriate timing of words, sentences, and the message as a whole;
- flexible, interesting, and authentic facial expressions.

These aspects of communication are part of conversation, not theatrical skills to be learned. But for many of us the naturalness of conversation is hard to maintain in the pulpit. To assess your current nonverbal patterns adequately, you need opportunities to see and hear your own voice and watch your own physical movements. Look at the material in the Appendix for further information. The more you enjoy yourself in preaching, the more your nonverbal behaviors will be appropriate to what you say as a worship leader.

The senses of sight, hearing, touch, taste, smell, and body movement are important to incorporate for worshipers as well as for as preachers during worship. Many worshipers receive cues from some but not all of these senses, so whenever you can offer more than one form of experience, the worship service becomes more accessible for more of the gathered community. For example, dance involves sound but does not depend on words. A cloth, an object, or a gathering of candles around the worship table can reinforce the preaching message.

> **Whenever you can offer more than one form of experience, the worship service becomes more accessible to more of the gathered community.**

Keeping a balance between attending to details and holding the vision of worship can be a challenge. Joseph Jeter of Brite Divinity School has cited an account from a novel by John McDonald (*The Scarlet Ruse*, Lippincott, 1980), that illustrates how hard it can be to lead worship and to worship at the same time. A viewer seated in the front row at a performance of a Spanish dance troupe was too much aware of the details and the machinery to enjoy the event—e.g., dancers' makeup smudged by perspiration, musicians slightly out of tune, and a curtain pulley showing from the side. Perhaps you have experienced similar struggles while seeing to the details of bringing people together in a worship setting. Taking time in silent prayer before and during worship may allow you to begin to breathe the Spirit again.

> **If you have been engaged in seeing to the details of bringing people together in a worship setting, you may have trouble listening to the Holy Spirit.**

Fred Craddock is perhaps the most widely beloved preaching mentor in the United States. He reported in a national preaching conference that he knew early in his ministry that he did not have the tall stature, resonant voice, or commanding gestures to achieve a traditional form of charisma for preaching. So, he reported, "I had to find some other way to say the Word that would fit me as I was." The result has been that he has encouraged thousands of other preachers to find their own voices and to tell the truth in and out of the pulpit.

Gender, Culture, and Worship Presence

As a child, I observed each Sunday morning our tall, thin, black-robed minister as someone who seemed different in almost every respect from me except for the pinkish color of our skin. I was sure the pastor was intelligent and dedicated to his calling. I could not imagine, however, that he had any of the questions I had, and I could not conceive of him falling off a bicycle and skinning his knee, as I often did. Part of the reason for this felt distance was the wide nonverbal difference between the two of us. This first pastor was a leader and a representative of the Church, but he did not evoke in me any identification with his life, his voice, or his situation outside the sanctuary.

Identification in the midst of differences is an issue in preaching across categories such as gender and culture. While preparing this book, for example, I received several written comments from female pastors with varying experiences in preaching. Their comments are a reminder that even with shifts in the number and characteristics of people entering congregational leadership, freedom in the pulpit is not always granted or claimed in

> *Identification in the midst of differences is an issue in preaching across categories such as gender and culture.*

the local church. Men more than women are expected to be the preachers in Sunday worship, and pastors are expected to be of the same racial or cultural background as their parishioners.

Authority for preaching is a matter for the preacher *and* the congregation. It is not automatic, and it requires discernment, dialogue, and prayer. In some worship settings women are perceived as giving talks instead of sermons. The reasons for this may have to do with both the vocal and verbal aspects of presence among many women preachers. Some of these can be differences in vocal pace, pitch, and emphasis; less use of argument and more use of observation and images; willingness to include personal testimony as part of the gospel message. As indicated by the three pastors' quotations below, freedom in preaching is a goal and a complex set of factors for those who preach and for those who respond to preaching in worship.

---

*My preaching professor helped me so much when he said,
"You do not need to preach like a man. Preach like Melanie,
and preach from the heart, and you will find your own voice."
That liberated me from trying to be someone I was not.*

Melanie

Authority in preaching is a tricky question. I feel I have it, but if the congregation does not award it to me, then what good does it do? I am merely preaching to myself. Perhaps the conclusion lies in the future.

Patricia

Pete, son of the church custodian, flatly stated, "No way a white woman can preach and meet the needs of a black congregation." Later, [after I had acknowledged that I could not be either white or male] members of the congregation came to me and said, "All anybody wants you to be is yourself. God will use you just as you are and that's plenty good for us." For a congregation to free a preacher to be himself or herself is a liberating gift.

Mallonee

The question of authority in preaching is a question of authenticity that affects men as well as women in the pulpit. When European American men are in leadership situations today, many people look for language and nonverbal cues that will indicate authenticity—i.e., avoiding or reversing the traditional images of the leader as certain, in control, and confident. At the same time, changes in preaching approach do not always bring about trust among listeners. For you as a preacher, in whatever circumstances, the pulpit can be a complicated place to present yourself as a leader with both integrity and authority.

Today you are challenged toward reality in the face of much unreal and damaging information about the world and those who communicate in public. As a congregational leader in worship, the first message you give to others when you preach or lead worship is that you are a creature in God's creation, part of the world that God loves and calls worthwhile. Your facial expressions, your voice modulations, your movements and gestures—all of these are gifts. As you grow in preaching you may increase your natural range of movements, vocal sounds, and facial experiences. Feedback from others will help in this continuing learning process, so that your own style of honoring the gospel will become increasingly comfortable and authentic.

The first time I was asked to preach in my home church was in seminary, [in a large church with a radio broadcast]. As I prepared I became quite nervous; terrified. My mother gave me a little advice. "Don't stand too close to the microphone when you sing. If you do they will hear you on the radio, and you don't sing well enough for that." Strangely enough those words gave me great comfort. My mother was not worried about my preaching; she had confidence in that. My mother

knew I had prepared well, practiced, and prayed. The wor
that I spoke were now up to God to use. It was my singin
that worried her. Since I currently preach not only to my c
gregation but to a radio audience, I take two steps back from
the microphone when the hymn begins.

Wayne

The Drama and Momentum of Worship

Worship is intended to transform its participants, including the preacher. When you lead or participate in a worship service, you may think of it first as a set of items placed in order during a set period of time. Worship can be much more than that: it is a process with its own integrity, flow, and momentum. The basic worship pattern in The United Methodist Church involves movement in time and space: gathering, hearing and proclaiming the Word, responding, giving thanksgiving and communion, and going forth. That worship pattern is a microcosm of the congregation's primary task of reaching out and receiving, helping people as they relate to God, nurturing them as a community of disciples, and sending them forth in service in the world. Paradoxically, worship at its best is both familiar and new. As a preacher, you have a crucial opportunity to share what you and others already know, and to bring about change in the midst of that knowing.

> **Paradoxically, worship at its best is both familiar and new. As a preacher, you have a crucial opportunity to share what you and others already know, and to bring about change in the midst of that knowing.**

> Where preaching has transforming effect, there is a giving and a taking of power. The one who listens holds power that can be given or withheld. The hearer can give or withhold that power. When it is given, the preacher is freed to go beyond recitation to proclaim truth with authority. In such a case the seed falls on fertile ground. If the hearer chooses to withhold power, holding back from the experience, building walls to close out any communication, the Word will be held back. The seed will fall on barren ground and will fail to bring fruit. . . . More hearers are ready to give that power than preachers are to claim it. There is a moment early in the preaching event in which some deep parts of the listener are opened up to the preacher as one is not routinely opened up to a neighbor or a friend or even a spouse. That moment is an invitation to transformation and an opportunity for a dialogue from depth to depth.
> Loren Mead, *Transforming Congregations for the Future,*
> Alban Institute, 1994, p. 56.

As a leader in worship, you are called to pay attention to the dynamic tension between the long view and the immediate view of the worship experience. Any given worship service is unique in time and space. You as an individual have changed from last week. The congregation has new experiences or struggles that emerge on this day. You are also part of something wider and deeper than any one word you may speak. You are given the chance to know, honor, and enjoy the cloud of witnesses across history and geography and across the aisle from you.

> *The freedom to preach grew out of a faithful, responsive relationship with the congregation. Out of the day-to-day life of the church and community I discovered an ever increasing level of openness and a willingness to grant me the freedom to speak the word as I sensed God was leading.*
>
> *John*

The concrete details of worship can help to foster the double gift of the immediate and the historic. You may wear a robe or an alb, symbolizing the priestly heritage of the worship leader or leaders. You may wear a stole or a cross that has been crafted for you by a member of the community, or carried from a distant place. The worship space around you may include cloth banners or musical instruments or memorial plaques. Each time you come into the worship space you have the chance to pay attention to these gifts of the senses. It can be tempting to take any one of these items for granted, but if you let them speak to you they provide a chorus of their own.

In my own local church in Nashville, a multiracial congregation in the heart of the city, Sunday worship often begins with a call to worship done in the call and response pattern used by our late associate pastor, Moses Dillard:

It is good—It is good—
To be in the house of the Lord—To be in the house of the Lord—
One more time—One more time!

For everyone who knew Moses prior to his death in 1993, the words celebrate his continuing presence as a beloved local saint. For others newer to the congregation, the words remind us that weekly worship tells our story and God's story each time we gather. Each time is new and special.

> *It may sound paradoxical, but I have discovered freedom in preaching by limiting myself to specific needs of specific persons. . . . I randomly pick out twelve persons from the attendance roll, write their names on individual 'post-its,' place them on the bulletin board above my computer screen, and then constantly check whether what I am preparing to preach has any relation to the need of the individuals listed. Each week, in other words, I have been surrounded by a great cloud of witnesses.*
>
> *Roger*

A spiritual discipline that frees me to preach is going into the sanctuary early Sunday morning—at least one hour before anyone else arrives. While there, I kneel at the altar and offer not only my words but myself to our gracious Lord in prayer. Then I spend some time 'waiting' in silence before the Lord, seeking God's anointing upon the worship time. I then take a 'Jericho walk' around the sanctuary in which I visualize the persons sitting in the pews, praying for many by name (remembering special concerns or events in their life at the moment). This prayer time concludes my preparation for participating with God in this awesome delight of preaching.

Dennis

Anything you do can become routine—even preaching. Recalling your first preaching moment can be helpful for the experienced preacher. Imagining yourself as part of a long company of dedicated and fallible persons can be helpful if you are concerned about your newness in the pulpit. Wherever you are located in the preaching pilgrimage, you are a worshiper.

How does the preacher experience God authentically? The question is important not only for keeping a pastor's inner life healthy, but also as a way to embody the Spirit of God in a congregation. You cannot decide at 9:55 A.M. Sunday to become a worshiper at 10:00 A.M. You need to have planned with others and allowed the work of all of you to feed into the celebration of worship. Cooperative planning is not a matter of a pastor handing a year's sermon titles to a musician on the one hand, and saying, "Fill in with appropriate anthems," or putting the titles and texts on a church secretary's desk and saying, "Fill in the prayers for the day." This is simply serial communication, and while it is not analogous to serial killing in its overt violence, it can be just as lethal to the presence of God in community.

> **You cannot decide at 9:55 a.m. Sunday to become a worshiper at 10:00 a.m. You need to have planned with others and allow the work of all of you to feed into the celebration of worship.**

Hospitality and Imagination

Preaching in worship is not always hospitable. The popular idiom "Don't you preach to me!" is a reminder that preaching is often seen as a complaint or a punishment. In keeping with our focus on the preacher as a person, however, hospitality toward yourself as well as hospitality toward worshipers is appropriate. Both new and experienced preachers can be inclined to see preaching as performance. If you center your attention on performing, you ask questions like, "Will I do well enough?" "What do the listeners consider a good job?" "What if I fail?" "What if I am not faithful to God's calling when I preach?"

> **Preaching that is hospitable can also be an event with a prophetic edge.**

A different way to consider preaching can free you from some of these questions. *Preaching is a gift from God to you, one that you have been given the chance to give to other people.* That makes preaching an act not of performance, but of hospitality. You are invited into the heavenly celebration and encouraged to open the door to others who may be waiting outside. Many people may not know what they are waiting for. You are offered a chance to name the waiting, the uncertainty, and with great joy the nature of the celebration they are invited to attend. You can claim each person in worship as an honored guest as you have discovered yourself to be.

Preaching that is hospitable can also be an event with a prophetic edge. Jesus' parable of the wedding feast tells of a banquet which the expected guests decided not to attend, making it an open festival for people from all walks of life and all personal circumstances. The later part of the story complicates the situation: a man who fails to come in proper wedding robes is turned away. This is not about a first century dress code, but about the need to recognize the heavenly festival as a prized blessing, worthy of your best discipline and respect. It makes no sense to receive the ultimate gift of God's grace—God's hospitality—and respond, "So—what else is new?"

In preaching classrooms and in seminars with preachers, I have found repeatedly that people change perceptibly when they tell a story that they have either lived through or observed for themselves. Their vocal range and enthusiasm increases, their movements are naturally connected with the words, and their eye contact with other persons increases as well. These phenomena are a major reason for pastors and others who preach to use directly experienced material rather than books of illustrations. Your imagination is engaged when you tell a story that matters to you.

> *I discovered freedom in preaching when I walked away from the pulpit and stood unprotected before the congregation, when I began telling stories, stories from my God-given creative talents based on Scripture, tradition, experience, and reason.*
>
> *Richard*

Similarly, people in the pews recognize truthful behavior when they see and hear it, even if they cannot label all the verbal and nonverbal cues using academic terms. They look for felt truth, for an encounter with reality that has more meaning for them than a closed, tidy little essay.

The Congregation and the Plumbline for Worship

The word often used for worship, *liturgy*, comes from the Greek word for the phrase *"the work of the people."* While you may think of preaching as the responsibility of the preacher, its source and power are in community. The ways you listen to each other and grow in your mutual understanding of God are at the heart of the Word spoken in worship. One image for this essential connection of the divine and the human is the *plumbline*. In terms of this book, the plumbline for preaching extends from the Spirit of God into the human community you encounter in worship and in daily experience. The quality of the plumbline depends on listening to God through prayer, Scripture, reading, and continuing dialogue with the people around you in a faith community. If you are an active worshiper, your ideas, activities, and imagination are part of that work of the people. If you are a preacher, your part in that work can be fruitful if you take the opportunity to enter into the worship experience jointly with others.

> **The quality of the plumbline depends on listening to God through prayer, Scripture, reading, and continuing dialogue with the people around you in the faith community.**

The phrase "Nice service, pastor," does not improve anyone's preaching. Fortunately there are better alternatives for communication between preachers and congregations. All presuppose an interest in preaching in the local church, and the belief that quality improvement in worship is appropriate to the work of God's people.

Here are several options for improving the quality of the congregational plumbline. Reflect on their possible uses in relation to your setting and leadership circumstances. You need not assume that others will be unwilling to participate. Many people are eager to be part of an active learning process.

<u>**Collaborative sermon formation and feedback**</u> processes give preachers and other leaders insights into the ways Scripture, daily life, and current experiences in the church are encountered by a variety of people. The conversation process involves having a group of persons selected by the pastor to serve as weekly discussion partners, using the lectionary or other designed readings for the worship services during a specified period such as two to four months. These processes can be powerful ways to increase the flow of information to preachers and to improve the connections of worshipers with each other. Don Wardlaw of McCormick Seminary has been developing these groups for many years, and John McClure reports a similar process in his book *The Roundtable Pulpit* (Abingdon, 1995).

<u>**Worship planning teams**</u> focus on the development of entire worship services, using either existing or ad hoc leadership in a local congregation. In some settings seasonal worship services are developed to include particular forms of proclamation, including drama, dialogue, and liturgical dance. In this context preaching becomes part of the larger drama of worship. *The United Methodist Book of Discipline – 1992* called for the first time for pastors and other worship leaders to plan worship together at least quarterly. This is less a regulation than an invitation to discover the natural synergy that occurs when people gather together in the Spirit.

<u>**Diary or journal 'listening' by a specified number of volunteers**</u> for a period of weeks can help a pastor recognize various people's current thoughts, events, and concerns in their daily life as the context for preaching preparation and as responses to preaching they have heard the prior week. This model is described by Roger Van Harn in *Pew Rights: For People Who Listen to Sermons* (Eerdmans, 1992).

<u>**Participative preaching during worship.**</u> Dialogue during preaching is possible when a preacher asks direct questions and hears the participants' responses as part

of the proclamation process. Particularly in smaller congregations and smaller worship spaces, the involvement of those present allows for a more conversational and less formal style of communication. This idea is described at length in Lawrence Wagley's *Preaching with the Small Congregation* (Abingdon, 1989).

In many African American congregations participation in preaching occurs as worshipers call out their approval, support, and/or challenge in words, movement, and applause, all of these forms of active listening that affect the energy of the celebration of worship. See for example Melva Wilson Costen's book *African American Christian Worship* (Abingdon, 1993).

Written feedback forms can be provided within a worship bulletin and turned in at the end of worship. Also, longer-term response forms can be developed to gather descriptive information about content, nonverbal factors, and thoughts and questions arising from preaching; this material can be used in a congregation over a period of time. (See the Appendix, pages 98-99, for one example of a response method and form.)

In all of these instances involving people in the local congregation, the work of the people can become creative beyond any one person's imagination. It is made possible by moving from isolation into community, and acting as the plumbline held ultimately by God.

QUESTIONS FOR REFLECTION

Consider these questions for your reflection and discussion with others.

1. In what ways is the worship in your local congregation multisensory? What senses are *least* apparent? How might your preaching influence this pattern?

2. What do you and other worship leaders do to examine and contribute to the drama, flow, and momentum of your worship? What do people say about those qualities in worship?

3. In what ways is your preaching hospitable? prophetic? engaging?

4. To what extent do you choose for worship stories you observe, stories you read, or stories you encounter yourself?

5. What is your approach to using manuscript, notes, or outlines in the pulpit? How do you practice using these materials? What could you change about this pattern?

6. How do you feel after a worship service is completed?

CHAPTER 5:
TOWARD THE WEST:
SUSTAINING THE COMMUNITY

From the West come purifying waters.
We pray that water might be pure and available to all,
and that we, too, may be purified
so that life may be sustained and nurtured
over the entire face of the earth.
(*The United Methodist Book of Worship*, no. 470.)

In the mythical past of American Western movies, every Easterner who went west had to be a pioneer. You never knew what life and death struggles lay ahead, because no one knew exactly what lay beyond the mountains or in the desert. For radio and then television heroes such as the Lone Ranger or Hopalong Cassidy, heroism continued to be seen as a noble and isolated calling. Even when there was a partner such as the Indian guide Tonto, the other person was an assistant, not an equal. More recently the central characters in what are called "action films" continue to maintain the premise that the lone hero—usually a Caucasian male—is to be admired and emulated. The fiction can be more powerful than fact.

What does this have to do with preaching and worship? Whatever its image in the past or as seen from a distance, preaching—as part of congregational leadership—is not a matter of riding into the sunset with music in the background. It is not always heroic. It is a matter of staying on a journey, one that may or may not sustain you depending on how you prepare, where you travel, and whether you make yourself available to appropriate partners.

> In a society and a world that have serious problems and suffer all too often and far too painfully from heartbreak, each of us needs a haven. Part of the touch of leadership is to create such a haven ....We know in our hearts that to be included is both beautiful and right. Leaders have to find a way to work that out, to contribute toward that vision.
>
> Max dePree, *Leadership Jazz*, Currency Doubleday, 1992, pp. 7, 63-64.

The Journey as Your Home

Christian educator Nelle Morton has written a book with a rich and telling title, *The Journey Is Home* (Beacon, 1986). In four words it gathers up the plot or thesis of this writing as a whole. When you leave a particular place, whether it has been a mountaintop or a dark valley, you will be changed as you continue to be on your way. If part of your life journey is to be preaching in Christian community, can you undertake the journey in such a way that it will stretch you and nourish you rather than dragging you down and sapping your strength? The premise of this section is that you will grow in your preaching if—I am inclined to say *only* if—you become proactive as a learner and teacher, particularly with other preachers. This is not to say that you cannot learn from other kinds of educational endeavors, but there is something in the preaching experience that is *uniquely personal and public*, bound by time and space yet going beyond either of them. To understand that uniqueness of experience in the company of others is to be freed for growth and transformation.

If part of your life journey is to be preaching in Christian community, can you undertake the journey in such a way that it will stretch you and nourish you rather than dragging you down and sapping your strength?

We humans need our lean-tos in the storms of life which come upon us when our bodies are too weary to work, our spirits are too hurt to struggle, and our hearts are too pained to care. The journey of the human spirit has tiring searches, long stretches of grief and letting go, dark-hearted things that steal the energy from our spirits. At these times we need lean-tos. Our lean-tos can be anyone or anything that brings us a sense of hope, a pause from the pain, a bit of strength to sustain us, a little vision for guidance, a touch of happiness. . . .We all need lean-tos; we all need to be lean-tos for others. . . . . Lean-tos are not permanent havens; they are temporary but essential shelters when the storms rage around us or inside of us. Becoming too dependent upon others is emotionally unhealthy. We need to trust others for comfort, support, and vision when our spirit feels weak and visionless, but in the end, we have to do our part, accept our responsibility, and make our own choices and decisions.

Joyce Rupp, *May I Have This Dance?*, Ave Maria Press, 1992, pp.42-43.

In many organizations during the last part of the twentieth century, the focus on quality has changed the language and landscape from an emphasis on *quality control* to an image of *continuing improvement*. In the church, particularly in The United Methodist Church, we are asking ourselves how we can respond to the world as both leaders and learners. Pastoral ministry was once assumed to be a leadership activity within the culture. Now, while there is less certainty about the role of the congregational leader, there is greater urgency that leaders have and articulate a vision for the people they serve. *At this period in time you cannot continue as a leader without being a learner.* This does not mean that you have to add formal education or degree programs to your schedule. It does mean that you will need to be in the process of discovering, examining, and sharing who you are and what you can become as an essential part of leading within Christian communities.

Living organisms are time-bounded entities. Their lives have beginnings, middles, and ends. But DNA, the most narcissistic of molecules, the molecule that carries life's intricate code, is able to create itself over and over again. Because living organisms replicate themselves, their endings are not as discrete as we might initially conclude. New forms are generated from the old; progeny carry into the future the cultural and genetic legacies of the previous generation. Endings are qualified, mitigated, blurred, by the beginnings that are left behind.

Dan McAdams, *Stories We Live By: Personal Myths and the Making of the Self*, William Morrow, 1993, p. 223.

Organic Learning

During the writing of this section of the book I had the chance to stay in a parsonage located one long block from the Pacific Ocean and another block from the only city intersection in Ocean Park, Washington. Being located in the midst of these two highly different vantage points, I found myself thinking about the *ecology* of preaching and worship. Ecology deals with the linking of organisms with their environments. The word *ecology* itself derives from the study of houses. The language of space connects with an experience in time. Similarly, how you continue to grow in your development as a preacher depends on where you are located (locating) and what kind of time is a framework for your experience. You may be writing the first actual sermon you have prepared. On the other hand, you may have used a particular pattern for preparing sermon manuscripts every Tuesday and Wednesday for many years. Or you may have a routine of letting the Word surround you for days until it comes together Saturday night. Any of those patterns can be valid. It is important, however, that you pay attention to the ways time and space influence your experience of preaching. Could you shift your ecological perspective from the microcosm to the macrocosm, and vice versa? What benefit might there be in that kind of shift? Here are two possibilities from two practicing preachers.

A radical concept of time is what sets my preaching free. . . . I believe that the preacher's eyes must encompass 10,000 years. Preaching is born out of a very deep memory of where we've been, and a certain eschatological excitement about our destiny, where we are going.

Norm

The psychologist Carl Rogers stated, "What is most personal is also most universal." This clearly applies to preaching. When we pastors are willing to discuss in living detail the deep joys, sorrows, and questions of life we erect strong bridges of understanding with our listeners. This openness invites an authenticity and honesty with oneself and God which creates a place for Christ to transform people at the core of their being.

David

Both of these preachers are reporting their individual perspectives of time and space. If they were members of the same group of preaching colleagues, their different angles of vision could contribute to a deepening awareness of the other's perspectives and perhaps open up new approaches for preaching. Dialogue can enable those present to hear God's word in new ways, enlarging their own preaching ministry and spiritual development.

Being a leader can imply not having to say you are vulnerable, but the truth is just the opposite. Realizing how much you depend on, learn from, and count on the life of other people is the gift of community. Discipleship cannot continue in isolation. For pastors and other congregational leaders, growth comes from shedding previous patterns of thinking, feeling, and adapting. The same is true for preaching. Having only one approach, one outline form, or one theme in your preaching will ensure that you burn out rather than stay alive and thrive.

Wherever you are located geographically, you are living on a frontier. The church exists in a wild and woolly, often frightening environment. The day of Christendom has passed, a time when people were presumed to be religiously active and public religion was embodied in our coins—"In God We Trust." Trust today is not automatically given to local churches or religious leaders. Alban Institute founder Loren Mead has said that "most of the national structures of the mainline churches are in shock, with a few giving signs of having moved to defensive retreat" (*Transforming Congregations for the Future*, Alban Institute, 1994, p. 112). Much energy is centered in personal experience, in television, or in local forms of safety rather than in national and global vision.

> **Wherever you are located geographically, you are living on a frontier. The church exists in a wild and woolly, often frightening environment.**

What does that have to do with you in your own situation? Quite simply, it means that learning is not just an individual matter but a national and international requirement for survival. The Church is the human species writ large, capable of drying up without food and moisture or growing into adulthood with appropriate nurture.

A friend who grew up in Minnesota describes the experience of being part of a small one-room schoolhouse. He learned something about many things, but he didn't learn very much about any particular item. He became good at helping younger siblings and neighbors learn, but he did not have his own learning muscles stretched. Helping others to learn is something we can celebrate. We also need to stretch ourselves and our partners in learning, so that the whole organism grows and improves while we learn.

There is a saying among biologists that "the only evidence of life is growth." The same holds true in human beings. Having something to learn, to try, to test, to communicate, makes the difference between atrophy and activity. You need not have daily or weekly contact with someone who is at the exact same life stage or educational level in order to have worthwhile dialogue about preaching. What is more essential is that you and others see yourselves as people with ideas and options, and that you be open to sharing your experience and allowing for dialogue from others.

> **What is essential is that you and others see yourselves as people with ideas and options, and that you be open to sharing your experiences and allowing for dialogue from others.**

Who can teach you? Whom can you teach? If you are new to preaching you may think it important not to let others view you as inexperienced. If you have been in preaching ministry for many years and are tired of old patterns, you may prefer not to let other people know of your low energy and diminished enjoyment for preaching and worship. In either case you may discover a major improvement in your own morale as you get to know more about what is facing people in other circumstances. New preachers can be high in energy but low in confidence. More experienced preachers can be less energetic but no less able to share their journeys and empathize with the struggles of their earlier days. *Learning among adults is not about rote practice but about renewing people.*

A Company of Preachers?

Developing yourself as a spiritual leader in worship asks that you be accountable to other persons over time. Whatever your initial training in preaching, you will not grow without the input, feedback, and support of other persons. Help from a family member is not enough. Written questionnaires about worshipers' responses can be of some assistance, but they cannot further your growth in the pulpit and in the congregation by themselves. Essential to thriving over time as a preacher is intentional connection and collegial support. Putting it in the biblical framework, Jesus' disciples were not found, taught, or sent out by themselves. Pairs, triads, and larger groups gathered to hear and do the Word, just as the early church gathered in homes and on the road to tell their stories. Though the Bible does not use the term *synergy*, it is clear that the gospel could not have spread without the synergic power of actively interdependent people.

> **Essential to thriving over time as a preacher is intentional connection and collegial support.**

> [U]sing synergic power means using our energy, talents, knowledge, and abilities to affect and influence the situation around us in order to co-create a more rewarding present and future for everyone. Synergic power is not possible without a sense of interdependence, which enables us to see that helping ourselves includes helping others. Synergic power is not displayed in a conflict of strength to see who wins. Instead it is used cooperatively, in conjunction with others, to see how the situation can be worked out to the benefit of all. Thus, with synergic power there are not "sides" to be pitted against each other.
>
> John Culley and Kristi Culley, *Be Not Conformed: Changing the Way We See the World*, Meyer Stone, 1989, p. 89.

Multiple forces work against collegial growth among preachers. They are similar to the forces that hinder cooperative, synergistic action among corporations, nations, and individuals. Particular hindrances to collegiality and synergy are individualism, competition, isolation, and perfectionism. All four are significant and pervasive; by naming them you can recognize their negative impact and strive to counteract it.

The concerns of individualism, competition, isolation, and perfectionism are identified here because they are tendencies to be identified rather than certainties to be assumed. Some pastors stay away from peer groups because they fear competition or future misunderstandings. On the other hand, some pastors decide that they need to counteract the competitive or perfectionist mindset that can come from isolation from their peers. A major premise of this writing is that developing in the preaching pilgrimage is better accomplished in the company of others than in separation from others. How you accomplish that development depends on your setting and your learning style. *Freedom to preach can come from freedom to discover your community for preaching.*

> Trusting people to be creative and constructive when given more freedom does not imply an overly optimistic belief in the perfectibility of human nature. It is rather a belief that the inevitable errors and sins of the human condition are far better overcome by individuals working in an environment of trust, freedom, and mutual respect than by individuals working under a multitude of rules, regulations, and restraints imposed upon them by another group of imperfect people.
>
> From the Kollmorgen Corporation annual report of 1979, quoted in Steven Covey, *First Things First: To Live, To Love, To Learn, To Leave a Legacy*, Simon and Schuster, 1994, p.264.

Survey researchers have reported that since the 1950s, more people in the United States express a fear of public speaking than report any other specific fear. A recent national report has highlighted another statistic related to communication and fear: an increasing percentage of adults—nearly half in a 1995 study—describe themselves as shy (Philip Zimbardo, reported in a National Public Radio interview, September 1995). You may not immediately connect preaching with shyness, but a significant number of pastors refer to themselves as introverts.

The role of congregational leader places people in a situation where the possible impact of their words is high and the risk of perceived inadequacy is large. While many pastors say they are comfortable with their peers, others report a hesitancy to trust others who are in the same district or Annual Conference. Where colleagues are likely over time to move into positions such as that of district superintendent, information about a pastor's struggles or confidential personal narratives can become problematic.

> *While many pastors say they are comfortable with their peers, others report a hesitancy to trust others who are in the same district or Annual Conference.*

- How do you decide whom to trust in the church?

- How does your spiritual development help you address that issue?

- Where does that issue have impact on the way you preach and the way you hear the gospel?

Those are the sorts of questions each of you can ask on your individual journey. In the meantime, here is a set of places where you might rest along the way.

Scenarios for Growth in Preaching

Each of the options described here has been used in actual settings around the United States. They do not exhaust the possibilities; they simply suggest alternatives that may fit your own circumstances. These suggestions offer you a mix of local, regional, and national approaches.

- A group of pastors decides to make a commitment to ongoing learning and sharing together in a regular, disciplined small group. They may model their work on any one of the following:

  ⇒ a lectionary study group, in which one person each time shares some research and responses to lectionary passages for a given week—a group that may be pastors of one denomination, an ecumenical pastor group, or a clergy-lay group;

  ⇒ a discussion and support group based on sharing sermon audio or video-tapes from the members' congregational worship services (for further information, see the Appendix, pages 95-99);

  ⇒ a Covenant Discipleship group led by a class leader, in which the members commit to ongoing efforts to improve and enrich their life as preachers, and to recount these experiences in the group setting.

- A group of interested persons plan a regular enrichment experience for pastors, entered on rich worship, good food, and time for personal sharing apart from administrative decision making.

- A group of regional staff and pastoral leaders develop a model for continuing learning in which large and small group sharing and preaching practice occur over several separate residential sessions. This effort requires developing processes to keep learners regularly in touch with each other and with new ideas for their work. Online computer networks may be available. This model originated in the United Methodist Academy for Preaching and has been adapted in several Annual Conferences.

- A pair of preachers agree to be partners in a mutual learning and growth process, talking regularly about their preaching ideas, sharing completed sermons with each other, and suggesting new approaches to material. (I have seen this model work with two pastors serving in different states who had mutual trust because of past years of working on the same staff. Their primary contact was through weekly long distance phone conversations, supplemented by face to face meetings when possible.)

- Individuals within the same district or cluster choose a group of three to five others with whom they want to develop a learning community, and they seek out learning resources and guides to mentor them.

- An individual finds a set of learning resources that will build on his or her continuing development. These can include books, video and audiotapes of teachers and pastors, study materials, and/or formal study such as a Doctor of Ministry program.

A mixture of the designs offered here may be appropriate for you and others in your environment. More important than any single model is the idea that you are part of a company of preachers, a congregation of those who serve as spiritual leaders. How you grow and thrive will influence both you and the communities around you.

> Being part of a community that is vision-driven is an unforgettable experience.
> Ezra Earl Jones, *Quest for Quality in the Church: A New Paradigm,* Discipleship Resources, 1993, p. 79.

QUESTIONS FOR REFLECTION

Consider these questions for reflection and discussion. Raise other issues as they emerge in your group setting.

1. What change or changes led you into preaching ministry?

2. Who are your heroes, in the church or in another context? Why do you choose them?

3. How do you experience sabbath time? Do you have to be forced to relax? What are your models for relaxing or for pushing on?

4. Is your congregation or your region of the church a high-trust or low-trust environment? How have you determined that to be true?

5. What is the present climate for collegiality among pastors? How might you influence that climate?

6. Where are the frontiers for your development as a spiritual leader?

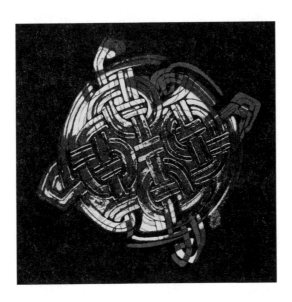

CHAPTER 6:

NAVIGATING THE FUTURE: THE CROSSING POINT AND THE SPIRAL

Paul reminds us that Christ is the center of creation,
    of our lives, and of the world.
We seek the wisdom of directions.
From each direction we return to the center
    reminded that Christ brings healing and salvation
    and by God's Spirit renews the face of the earth.
Let us be silent as we face our center.
          (*The United Methodist Book of Worship*, no. 470)

During a preaching seminar in Tacoma, Washington, I asked several dozen people what they were looking for in relation to their preaching. The first person said, "I'm Tom, and this is my first year in the local church. I hope to stay alive in preaching for at least the next thirty years." A few minutes later another pastor said, "I'm John, and I've *been* preaching for thirty years. I'd like to stay alive as a preacher for many more years." Then Susan spoke, saying "I'm a lay speaker, and I'm new to preaching. I'd like to become more confident that what I preach is true and worth the telling." Their histories were different, but their goals for developing in the art and craft of proclaiming the Word were essentially the same. They all were hoping for continuing growth and renewal.

In writing this book I have been driven by an awareness of metaphors of space and time. Even the term "driven" implies a mixture of the two: I have been on the road into FREEDOM IN THE PULPIT for quite a while. Perhaps the inclination to keep referring to spatial and temporal language simply shows that preaching is a natural process. Whether you are getting ready to preach or listening to another person preach, you are doing a kind of communicating that is rooted in the human need to connect and to make a difference in your surroundings.

Compass and Crossing Point

The two basic directions or trajectories of the Christian faith are often referred to as the horizontal—focusing on the relation of humans with each other; and the vertical —focusing on the relation of God and human beings. The Compass Model used as the framework for much of this book is compatible with that basic notion in one respect; we have been looking at both the spiritual and the social dimensions of our faith development as hearers and doers of the gospel. Bishop Earl Hunt affirms this essential connection.

> If we believe in a holistic evangelism, it will always have two dimensions: the vertical, symbolizing a person's relationship to God; and the horizontal, having to do with a person's relationship to his or her fellow human beings. Thus, in a very real way, Christian evangelism at its best is both personal and social.
> Bishop Earl G. Hunt, Jr., *Evangelism for a New Century: The 1994 Denman Lectures*, Discipleship Resources, 1994, p. 54.

At the same time this book is intended to encourage you to push the boundaries of the vertical/horizontal frame of reference. I do not encounter a separation or opposition of one dimension with the other in daily life. Many of the people you meet inside or outside the church do not experience that separation either. What is more important is how the integrity, the wholeness of person and community, emerges, and how the work we do as laypersons and pastors, preachers and spiritual leaders can add to that wholeness as the Body of Christ. Again think of the idea of discipline and freedom as interwoven processes. Moving into, through, and at the same time beyond the preaching process is an important way to keep your bearings and develop the leadership potential for the whole community. James and Evelyn Whitehead affirm the idea of a sacred partnership as an image of renewing and freeing leadership.

> [T]he religious leader is not separate from the community, invested with powers that other Christians utterly lack. The leader's actions do not replace our own; rather, they remind us of our responsibility. . . . A community of faith designates its leader as a mediator—one who stands between. Mediator is an enduring image in Christian life, but it survives today only by being transformed. The role of mediator changes as our view of our religious world shifts. In a hierarchical world we pictured God as transcendently beyond and above us. Such a worldview elevates our leaders, placing them above the community, between God and the rest of us. In the world of mutuality that Christians are reclaiming these days, we understand mediation differently. No longer living in a vertical world, we do not picture our leaders above us. Leaders are our partners in faith, not our parents or rulers.
>
> James D. Whitehead and Evelyn Eaton Whitehead, *The Promise of Partnership: A Model for Collaborative Ministry*, Harper-SanFrancisco, 1991, pp. 132-134.

A paradox lies at the heart of the process I have been describing throughout this book. Amid the words necessary for describing good preaching there is the equally important reality of silence. The centering prayer includes in its first stanza the words,

"Let us be silent as we face our center point." Later, as worshipers come back to the center, the last verses suggest again a need to be silent and listen:

If we walked a path in each direction, the sacred paths would form a cross.
Returning to the center, we discover Christ, who calls us and challenges us.

For any of us who hope to speak the Word faithfully, silence and listening are essential gifts of the Spirit.

In the earlier sections of the book the compass directions served as ways of reflecting on the continuing journey that I call the preaching pilgrimage. That journey can be entered at any point; all of the directions have their own meaning and value. There is one further aspect of this symbolic journey, however, that deserves mentioning. As I indicated earlier in the section "Toward the South," the vertical connection of the Spirit of God and the Body of Christ serves as the congregational plumbline. The horizontal connection, that of preparing the Word and sustaining yourself and others in community, seems to be equally important, for it is the line of intentional commitment to growth and improvement. These two come together in a crossing point. This crossing point is of course a metaphorical equivalent to the cross. The figure below represents this process.

THE CROSSING POINT

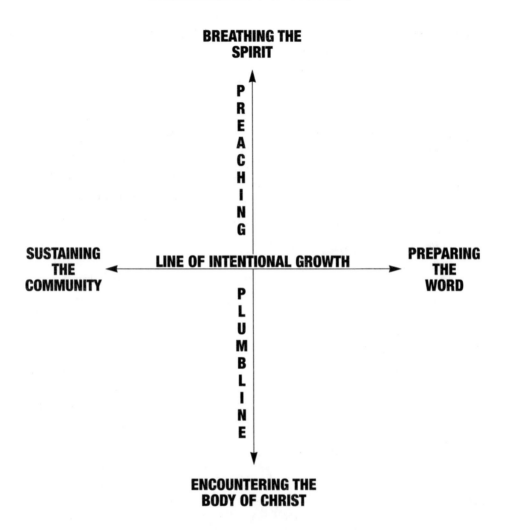

**BREATHING THE
SPIRIT**

P
R
E
A
C
H
I
N
G

**SUSTAINING
THE
COMMUNITY** ← **LINE OF INTENTIONAL GROWTH** → **PREPARING
THE
WORD**

P
L
U
M
B
L
I
N
E

**ENCOUNTERING THE
BODY OF CHRIST**

To be a preacher is at some level impossible, because human words cannot convey all of the meaning in what we refer to as Cross or Resurrection or the Realm of God. But this image of the crossing point suggests that there is hope in the process.

Moving into a Spiral Flow

What makes preaching in a Christian community powerful and at the same time humbling is that you and I cannot tell the whole Christian story at any one moment, and we do not control the outcomes of worship. We can only navigate, to use yet another space/time metaphor. The waters constantly change around us, and we use instruments that are finite and fallible: ourselves and our experiences of the gospel. That is the limitation in what we do, but it is also the certainty of God's grace that allows us to do this strange, wonderful task. I have used a computer to write this text, but the computer is merely a tool for making other things happen in the power of God.

As this writing moves to a close, I shift from the spatial metaphor of the compass toward a spatial/temporal metaphor, *the spiral*. Writing about something that has duration but not finality is a paradox, even a contradiction. But there is something to be named and claimed beyond what we do individually when we grow in preaching. We breathe the Spirit, prepare the Word, encounter the Body of Christ, and hope to sustain community—all natural processes in the vocation of hearing and speaking the gospel. At the same time we do not and cannot control the results when the Word of God goes forth in us and through us into the world. It goes beyond what any one of us can produce. I invite you to think of your time in preaching as an expanding spiral, beginning from your first remembered experiences, and extending into your present and future as person, pilgrim, and preacher.

> **We do not and cannot control the results when the Word of God goes forth in us and through us into the world. It goes beyond what any one of us can produce.**

Preaching in worship is a way to embody spiritual, visionary leadership in the local congregation. This can occur in a myriad of forms, in multiple voices and faces and settings. It is impossible to find a single set of correct words for the rich encounter of the person preaching, the preached Word, the drama of worship, and the gathered community. These words do not cover the territory. Something of the order of *flow* leads any one of these ideas or experiences to spill over into the others. The words of Scripture give us guidance. You can imagine the symbols of abundance or flow in the biblical narratives—the oil running down over the beard of Aaron in Psalm 133, the cup overflowing in Psalm 23, the father's joyous run toward his lost son in Luke 15, and the scattering of the seeds in Mark 4. Abundance, not scarcity, is characteristic of the reign of God.

> **Preaching in worship is a way to embody spiritual, visionary leadership in the local congregation.**

As you consider your present and future life in behalf of Christian community, you can count on the door being open to growth and possibility, even in the midst of problems and difficulties. The Word will not leave you empty, a truth that countless preachers have affirmed.

For me preaching is a corporate experience. When I realize that God's Holy Spirit is active throughout the event—in the mind and spirit of the preacher but also in the lives of members of the congregation—preparing the soil of human souls for the seeds of God's Word, then I know the freedom implied in the title of this resource. I am free to preach because God has already done the hard work of stirring souls—mine and others'—to receive God's Word.

Charles

The Gospel of John echoes that affirmation in Scripture:

> Then Jesus said to the Jews who had believed in him,
> "If you continue in my word, you are truly my disciples;
> and you will know the truth, and the truth will make you free."
>   John 8:31-32 (NRSV)

Fragments of Maps for Navigating

There are many potential applications of this navigation into the future. Here are several that are currently becoming visible and worth noting in the Church.

1. As churches become more diverse and more global, you will come to know about and celebrate **cultural traditions in preaching and worship**: the Korean prayer tradition, for example, the fiesta worship in many Spanish language churches, and the African American call and response pattern interweaving music and preaching. We can be free to enjoy different gifts available in the varying approaches to vital worship, not as token examples for special Sundays but as ways to expand awareness of communities across time and space.

2. **Contemporary or alternative worship** is a phrase used to suggest a wide-spread concern to unite evangelism and worship through relevant and inviting experiences of Christian community. Freedom in proclaiming the gospel in alternative settings may include drama, dance, and other media. Preaching can be done in a variety of ways that welcome seekers into new worship experiences. The key is that a preacher be able and willing to embody the freedom of the gospel in an authentic way. Important as the trappings of alternative worship may seem to be, costuming and context are less important than the authentic voices of caring communicators.

3. **Renewal of interest in preaching** is apparent in the United States and in other countries. The interest has led to a great many written and audiovisual resources about preaching. As I indicated in the section on "Preparing the Word," discerning which resources lead to strengthening the preacher's freedom to preach remains an important question. The increase of interest in preaching signals at the very least a recognition of the power described in Isaiah 55:11b-12. God affirms through the prophet not only the effectiveness but the joy inherent in preaching God's Word.

> "It shall not return to me empty, but it shall accomplish that
> which I purpose, and succeed in the thing for which I sent it.
> For you shall go out in joy, and be led back in peace;
> the mountains and the hills before you shall burst into song,
> and all the trees of the field shall clap their hands."
>   (Isaiah 55:11b-12, NRSV)

More and more pastors and denominational leaders are looking for ways to help preachers develop spiritually, focusing on the *formation* of persons who lead congregations as a *continuing foundation* for their present and future ministries.

The Two Stories

> [W]e finally do not know—we do not really know—when preaching is effective. Surely every experienced pastor has had occasions when people have said how much they were helped or changed by a sermon that the pastor had quite forgotten, or remembers with embarrassment. We do not know what is happening in this encounter called preaching. There is a great mystery involved. But the awareness of the mystery dare not be an excuse for neglecting the mastery of which we are capable. Our final reliance is on the promise that the Word shall not return void; our present obligation is to employ and refine every gift in our possession as we help in sending it forth on its mission.
>
> Richard John Neuhaus, *Freedom for Ministry*, revised ed., Eerdmans, 1992, p. 184.

Through a decade of working with both new and experienced preachers, I have heard on a regular basis two separate narratives that could both be called stories of "sermon failure."

Failure Story #1

(You may not initially believe that the first story is about a preacher's failure. Continue reading.)

Preacher J has worked hard and long on a sermon that seemed until the moment of worship to be a wonderful, pleasing message, one of which this preacher could be proud. But in the moment of preaching that message, Preacher J notices that no one's eyes look brighter, no heads have nodded in agreement, no smiles or even frowns signal an active response in the making. After worship, the parishioners offer their traditional handshake and "Nice service," but it is clear that nothing of importance has happened among them. Preacher J leaves the church building, wondering whether all that work was for nothing.

Failure Story #2

Preacher K has spent all week putting out fires and holding hands in the local congregation: three difficult meetings, counseling with a family coming unglued, and the funeral of a child killed in an accident. A quick glance at the lectionary passages while at the hospital is done so that a bulletin can be typed. There has been no time at all to stop and think about the skimmed passages. Late Saturday night the exhausted Preacher K considers grabbing from the shelf a sermon by Billy Graham or Peter Marshall, just to have something to say the next day. But that won't work either. The bulletin is already printed, and Preacher K does not read other people's material aloud very well. So a brief, simpleminded story is told in an attempt at preaching. K tries to get out the door quickly, hoping to forget this terrible week and be forgiven. In the vestibule one parishioner after another comes forward and grasps Preacher K's hand, saying, "How did you *know* that I was going through that struggle?" and "This was *exactly* what I needed to hear today!" Preacher K walks back home, quietly reflecting on the unpredictability of preaching and the strangeness of the gospel.

> We are each of us the prodigal, needing to hear God, needing to return to [God], to come home to those welcoming and forgiving hands held out to us, to the place where we most truly belong. This is the universal human experience.
>
> Esther deWaal, *A Seven Day Journey with Thomas Merton,* Servant Publications, 1992, p. 34.

The preaching pilgrimage is evidence of the Spirit of God at work in the world. Each time you move through the compass points of breathing the Spirit, preparing the Word, encountering the Body of Christ, and sustaining the community of those who preach and lead, you are expanding the reign of God within you and around you. The spiral is a symbol of that ongoing process. It has no definite endpoint, because you as preacher and pilgrim have none. The work goes on, the celebration continues, and the life of which you are part is everlasting.

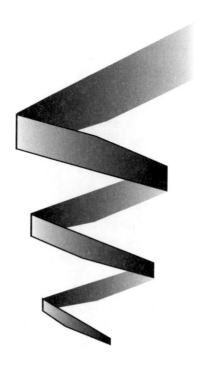

QUESTIONS FOR REFLECTION

Here are questions for reflection and discussion concerning navigating your future in preaching. They are intended to open but not exhaust the possibilities for your thinking.

1. In what way do you see yourself evolving or changing intentionally as a preacher? What are the elements, as you are aware of them, leading to this result?

2. What helps keep you from losing your compass and getting lost? Are those resources sufficient?

3. What balance exists for you between the vertical and the horizontal dimensions of experience? In the life of the congregation you know best?

4. Where are the most reliable growth-producing experiences in your life and ministry?

5. How are you fostering the growth of other leaders and preachers?

6. What are your images of the future, for yourself, for your congregation, for your denomination, for the world? How comfortable are you with these images?

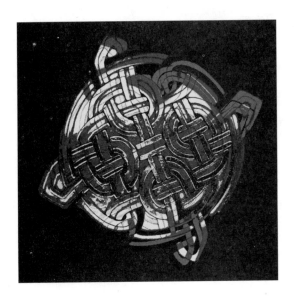

APPENDIX:

VIDEO AND AUDIO FEEDBACK
FOR PREACHING GROWTH

However good a communicator you may be, feedback from videotaping or audiotaping your own and others' preaching can improve your effectiveness and increase your enjoyment of preaching. Presented here are the rationale, methods, and applications for a teaching-learning tool which is also—often surprisingly—a major resource for the preacher's spiritual formation as well. From more than two decades of using videotape feedback in particular, I am convinced that it can nurture as well as challenge people.

In videotaping preaching segments or whole sermons, the preacher has a chance to see and hear the proclamation as an observer and receiver. The results are powerful in combination with the verbal feedback of a group of preaching colleagues, particularly over a period of time. Self-knowledge adds comfort, and the safety of knowing your preaching style can more fully aid in your ability to develop or change patterns of language and movement.

Context and Rationale for Videotaping of Preaching

The model I have found useful in both seminary classes and pastors' meetings has several important features.

If videotaping preaching in the group setting, two or three persons read their chosen Scripture passage followed by their preaching segment. (You may choose part or all of a sermon, depending on time availability. Beginning with the first five minutes can work well.) No notes are taken during the preaching. A pause of two or three minutes allows the listeners of each sermon to make brief notes on a form such as supplied on pages 98-99. After the two or three preachers have been heard and time allowed for written notations, a break is taken by the group as a whole.

After the break, each preacher begins by sharing a brief comment about his or her experience in this session—reactions, concerns, surprises. This allows the respondents to take note of the speaker's level of comfort or discomfort and often removes the necessity for others to refer to the preacher's nervousness. Experiencing anxiety tends to bother new preachers more than it does worshipers, who usually perceive nervousness as a sign of earnestness about the important task of preaching. Other group members then share their experiences of the preaching, in two stages:

- first, what they have received (the gifts of the sermon, recounted from a personal perspective: "I heard—I noticed—I imagined," and so forth); and
- second, what could help them to hear or retain the message even better.

Each preacher is a listener to the responses to his/her own message and a respondent to the next person's message. It is important to *cluster* the initial messages in a single teaching/learning session because the feedback to the first preacher can be distracting for the next preacher and can move the session as a whole beyond its scheduled time. The intention in clustering the messages is to recognize valid and creative differences in preaching approaches, and to convey that preaching "in the company of the saints" builds up the wider company of preachers as spiritual leaders.

After the feedback conversation is completed, the preacher is encouraged to watch the videotape with at least one other person. Reasons for this choice are that persons do not always hear the full import of the positive feedback they receive. A careful observer may be able to spot moments of special power and effectiveness, when the words and the personal manner or style come together particularly well. Many times both newer and more experienced preachers become intent on their nonverbal mannerisms and fail to notice their moments of great power—unless they are invited to take note of them by a caring colleague.

If done well, this process can be formative and enjoyable for everyone concerned. Several cautions are in order.

1. **The words *feedback*, *critique*, and even *evaluation* evoke defensive postures among many if not most adults.** The only way to counter defensiveness is for a facilitator and the participants to commit themselves to <u>discovering the gifts</u> in each person's preaching and committing themselves jointly to the best efforts possible.

2. **Responding to preaching is a form of preaching in itself.** As in the local congregation, telling a person "What you should have said" is less likely to

build trust and promote growth than descriptions of the listener's own reaction and concrete examples of what behaviors worked well. The same is true for other worshipers: direct description ("I experience Christ's presence in this place!") brings people into the circle, while the imperative can do the opposite ("Change or get out!")

3. **Videotaping in a classroom or seminar setting is admittedly limited because it fails to show the multisensory and community-based features of corporate worship.** It is helpful to recognize these limits but to recognize at the same time that the Word can be made flesh in any setting. Classmates or other colleagues need to hear the Word of God as much as anyone. Preaching can be "real" even if it is not in a traditional worship space.

4. **Videotaping a worship service can be helpful if it can be done without detracting from the worship.** Apart from the worship service proper, a video camera can be set up so that the preacher can see and hear worship leaders in the local setting. Liturgists and other worship leaders can also observe their patterns as a means of developing worship flow and momentum together.

Audiotaping of Preaching

In many congregations audiotapes are given or sent to people not able to attend corporate worship. For this reason, discovering the pitch, pace, clarity, and intensity of your voice are important features of your outreach. Another benefit of audiotaping preaching is the option of circulating preaching audiotapes among a group of preaching colleagues. When pastors or lay speakers are geographically isolated from one another, you can send cassette tapes of each other's preaching to your colleagues, and listen to them in your automobiles.

One approach to audiotaping preaching is a round robin model. In this model the preparation notes and sermon by one preacher can be heard by others and audio responses recorded by those respondents; then the responses are sent back to the original preacher for further discernment or dialogue. (This is similar to the Circuit Rider Sermon Series used by the United Methodist Publishing House for a number of years.) One potential advantage of arranging this kind of round robin is that you can be sharing preaching ideas and responses with a group of colleagues over a period of time, then following up on this process with a joint session that includes video feedback and sharing of insights from your mutual work. The key is to adapt your use of audio and video to your own geography, congregational context, and goals for growth.

WORKSHEET FOR RESPONDING TO PREACHING

This form can be used by receivers of preaching in congregational or small group settings. Comments are given to the preacher for later reference.

1. When were you most engaged with this person's message?

2. What seems to be the central idea or direction of this message?

3. How would you describe this preacher's style, both verbal and nonverbal?

4. Which of the three worlds of preaching do you experience most clearly here—the Scripture, the community, the preacher? Do you find them all to be present?

5. What response is called forth in you by this sermon?

6. What would help you enjoy, remember, or apply this preacher's message more effectively?

7. What other thoughts do you have about this experience?

Name of the preacher: Respondent:

You are asked to be descriptive, not judgmental. Focus on present gifts and potential growth, rather than "weaknesses."

A Select List of Materials on Preaching

Burghardt, Walter J., S.J. *Preaching: The Art and the Craft.* Paulist, 1987.

Buttrick, David. *Homiletic.* Augsburg Fortress, 1987.

Craddock, Fred B. *Preaching.* Abingdon, 1985.

_____. *Overhearing the Gospel.* Abingdon, 1978.

_____. *As One Without Authority.* Abingdon, 1971, 1978.

Davis, Donald. "Four Crises in Preaching." Videotape produced by the Worship Unit of The General Board of Discipleship, 1992.

Donders, Joseph G. *Praying and Preaching the Sunday Gospel.* Orbis, 1988.

Elkins, Heather Murray. *Worshiping Women.* Abingdon, 1995.

González, Justo L., and González, Catherine G. *Liberation Preaching: The Pulpit and the Oppressed.* Abingdon, 1980.

Lowry, Eugene. *Living with The Lectionary.* Abingdon, 1992.

_____. *The Homiletical Plot.* Abingdon, 1980.

_____. *Doing Time in the Pulpit.* Abingdon, 1985.

McClure, John. *The Roundtable Pulpit: Where Leadership and Preaching Meet.* Abingdon, 1995.

Meyers, Robin. *With Ears to Hear: Preaching as Self-Persuasion.* Pilgrim, 1993.

Mitchell, Henry. *Celebration and Experience in Preaching.* Abingdon, 1990.

O'Day, Gail, and Long, Thomas G., eds. *Listening to the Word: Studies in Honor of Fred B. Craddock.* Abingdon, 1993.

Schlafer, David J. *Surviving the Sermon: A Guide to Preaching for Those Who Have to Listen.* Cowley, 1992.

_____. *Your Way with God's Word: Discovering Your Distinctive Preaching Voice.* Cowley, 1995.

Staying ALIVE in the Pulpit! Series One and Two. Teaching Videos from the Academy for Preaching. Discipleship Resources and EcuFilm, 1994 and 1995.

Taylor, Barbara Brown. *The Preaching Life.* Cowley, 1993.

Thulin, Richard. *The "I" of the Sermon.* Augsburg Fortress, 1989.

Troeger, Thomas H. *The Parable of Ten Preachers.* Abingdon, 1992.

_____. *Imagining a Sermon.* Abingdon, 1990.

Wardlaw, Don M., ed. *Preaching Biblically: Creating Sermons in the Shape of Scripture.* Westminster/John Knox, 1983.

Wilson, Paul Scott. *The Practice of Preaching.* Abingdon, 1995.

_____. *Imagination of the Heart.* Abingdon, 1988.

List of Illustrations and Tables

List of Names

The publisher gratefully acknowledges permission to reprint the following copyrighted material:

Frederick Buechner: From Listening to Your Life: Daily Meditations with Frederick Buechner. San Francisco: Harper, 1992. Used with permission from Harriet Wasserman Literary Agency.

Stephen R. Covey. Reprinted with the permission of Simon & Schuster from First Things First by Stephen R. Covey, A. Roger Merrill, and Rebecca R. Merrill. Copyright © by Stephen R. Covey, A. Roger Merrill, and Rebecca R. Merrill.

Fred B. Craddock: From Preaching. Nashville: Abingdon, 1985. Used with permission of the author.

John and Kristi Culley: From Be Not Conformed: Changing the Way We See the World. New York: Meyer Stone Books, 1989. Used with permission of the authors.

Max dePree: From Leadership Jazz. New York: Currency/Doubleday, 1992. Used with permission from Doubleday.

Esther deWaal: From A Seven Day Journey with Thomas Merton. Ann Arbor: Servant Publications, 1992. Used with permission from Servant Publications.

Robert Fulghum: From From Beginning to End: The Rituals of Our Lives. New York: Villard Books/Random, 1995. Used with permission from Random House.

Earl G. Hunt, Jr.: From Evangelism for a New Century: The 1994 Denman Lectures. Used with permission from Discipleship Resources, Nashville, TN.

Ezra Earl Jones: From Quest for Quality in the Church: A New Paradigm. Used with permission from Discipleship Resources, Nashville, TN.

Eugene L. Lowry: From Doing Time in the Pulpit: The Relationship Between Narrative & Preaching. Nashville: Abingdon Press, 1985. ©1994, Eugene L. Lowry.

Dan McAdams: From Stories We Live By: Personal Myths and The Making of the Self. New York: William Morrow, 1993. Used with permission from William Morrow.

Loren Mead: Reprinted from Transforming Congregations for the Future with permission from The Alban Institute, Inc., Suite 433 North, 4550 Montgomery Avenue, Bethesda, MD 20814. Copyright ©1994. All rights reserved.

Robin R. Meyers: From With Ears to Hear: Preaching as Self-Persuasion ©1993. Used with permission of Pilgrim Press, Cleveland, Ohio.

Stephen Nachmanovitch: From Free Play. New York: Jeremy P. Tarcher, Inc., 1990. Used with permission from The Putnam Publishing Group.

Richard Neuhaus: From Freedom for Ministry, revised edition, Wm. B. Eerdmans Publishing Co., ©1992. Used with permission of the publisher.

Eugene H. Peterson: From The Contemplative Pastor: Returning to the Art of Spiritual Direction. Grand Rapids: Eerdmans Publishing Co., 1989. Used with permission of the publisher.

Joyce Rupp: From May I Have This Dance?. Copyright ©1992 by Ave Maria Press, Notre Dame, IN 46556. Used with permission of the publisher.

Norman Shawchuck and Roger Heuser: From Leading the Congregation by Norman Shawchuck and Roger Heuser. Copyright ©1994 by Abingdon Press. Used with permission of the publisher.

Margaret Wheatley: From Leadership and The New Science, copyright ©1992 by Margaret Wheatley, Berrett-Koehler Publishers, Inc., San Francisco, CA. All rights reserved. Reprinted with permission of the publisher.

James D. Whitehead and Evelyn Eaton Whitehead: From The Promise of Partnership by James D. Whitehead and Evelyn Eaton Whitehead. Copyright ©1991 by Whitehead Associates. Reprinted with permission of HarperCollins Publishers, Inc.